Our Fathers who art in heaven

and what they continue to teach us

Gerry Murak

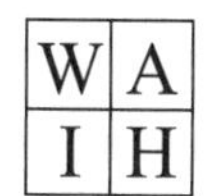

WAIH Publishing

05 06 07 08 09 HH 5 4 3 2 1
First Edition
Printed in the United States of America
ISBN 10: 0-9759057-1-6
ISBN 13: 978-09759057-1-6
OCC019000 Self-Help/Inspirational
Library of Congress Control Number: 2005925614
$17.95 U.S. Funds

Requests for permission to make copies of any part of this work can be made to:

OFWAIHF
P.O. Box 502
Getzville, NY 14068

Our Fathers Who Art in Heaven Foundation
1-866-OFWAIHF
info@OFWAIHF.org

Cover design by Andrew Murak, Copyright ©2005.
Book design by Cameo Publications, LLC.

"Every father's soul lives in you, and *Our Fathers Who Art In Heaven* makes it shine, glow, and warm your heart."

– Mark Victor Hansen,
co-creator of the *Chicken Soup for the Soul®* series

"*Our Fathers Who Art in Heaven* is a source of inspiration for anyone who has lost their father."

– John Gray, Ph.D.
author of *Men Are from Mars, Women Are from Venus*

"Fathers are the carpenters of the soul. This book reveals that better than any other written to date. Read it and add another room to store memories in your soul."

– Yvonne Divita, President and Founder,
Windsor Media Enterprises & WME Books

"Some of the greatest joys in life come when we recall the precious moments when our dads shared their love and wisdom with us. If you want to relive those glorious moments more often, then you must read this book. It is a keeper."

– Bud Gardner, co-author,
***Chicken Soup for the Writer's Soul®*,**
a *New York Times* Bestseller

"Men of glory, men of principle and virtue, men of simplicity, yet heroic and moving!"

– Oliver Young (Yang Hanfeng),
Manager of Investor and Public Relations,
PetroChina Company Limited, Beijing, China

"Don't read this book – unless you want a big lump in your throat and a sense of déjà vu as you reflect on your own life lessons learned at your dad's knee, workbench, or desk. A powerful reminder of how family marks our lives forever."

– Dianna Booher, author of more than 40 books,
including *Your Signature Life and Your Signature Work*

"This book commemorates the memories of our departed dear fathers and their teachings till eternity."

– Gopal Krishan Puri, CEO, IIMS Publications, India,
renowned author of 150 books

"For so many years, Dad and I played together, learned together, and worked together. Today, we only get to talk together when I sleep. Thanks to *Our Fathers Who Art in Heaven*, that conversation is much more lively and refreshed! Thanks to Gerry for helping me rekindle that warm feeling!"

**– Rick Duha, Managing Director,
The Duha Group, Winnipeg, Manitoba, Canada**

"*Our Fathers Who Art In Heaven* fills a real need for people who have lost their fathers and are looking for some inspiration from others who have traveled the same road. Gerry has found a wonderful way to explore the relationships we have with our fathers and the legacies they leave us."

**– Mark Simon, CEO & Executive Director,
Western New York Upstate Transplant Services**

"Gerry Murak's book touches a part of us that everyone shares. It brings out feelings that will bring comfort, tears, laughter, and memories, no matter what kind of relationship you had with your father. Rarely does a book make you feel so good about being a part of the human race."

– Joe Calloway, author of *Becoming a Category of One*

"The 'Spirit' of my father still floats throughout our company. We feel it, embrace it, and do all we can to carry his business philosophies on even after his passing. It is refreshing to hear that others know what I am feeling as well."

–Rick McIntosh, President, MAC's Antique Auto Parts

"Leadership and wisdom are subjects that have been considered from the time of the ancients through today. Gerry Murak brings a fresh perspective to the subject in his new book, which shares insights deceased fathers have left to their children. Real life lessons for real people. A wonderful concept!"

**–Scott E. Friedman, Partner,
Lippes Mathias Wexler Friedman LLP, author of
The Successful Family Business and *How to Run a Family Business***

"*Our Fathers Who Art In Heaven* is a testimonial to those fathers on whose shoulders we now stand! These stories are real life experiences that speak to all of us about life, purpose, and challenge."

– Frank C. Bucaro, speaker, business ethics expert, and author of *Taking The High Road – How To Succeed Ethically When Others Bend the Rules* and *Trust Me! Insights into Ethical Leadership*

"A personalized learning experience. By engaging us in searching for lessons in our own experiences, Gerry seeks both to make us our own teachers and to honor a generation of fathers who worked hard and realized dreams for themselves and their families."

– Theodore A. Beringer, Chairman & CEO, Beringer & Company

"Everyone has a father. Some of us had a close relationship with him, while others may have never known him. This book reads like a touching memoir, rich with vivid memories."

– Rosemarie Rossetti, Ph.D., speaker, trainer, consultant, author of *Take Back Your Life*, and President, Rosemarie Speaks, A Rossetti Enterprises Inc. Company

"I've been blessed with the opportunity to work with my father for the past 18 years. His experience and wisdom is offered to me daily, a gift I do not take for granted. These stories ground me solidly to that purpose. Thanks for sharing these lessons. Their truths resonate and honor the men that made us."

– Ken Shuman, President, Shuman Plastics

"This book isn't about deceased fathers; it's about fathers who have left lasting impressions that will now be passed on for generations."

– Pam Lontos, President, PR/PR

"I have not found a guide book on being a dad…until now. Every dad needs to read this and get copies for their sons…stories about real dads that inspire, inform, and teach us about the critical role of being a father."

– Stan Craig, pastor, author of *Legacy Leadership*, speaker, and dad

“What a gem this is! Gerry Murak has given us ‘more than a shovel-full’ of sweet remembrances and lessons learned from those good men who have gone before us.”

– Lou Heckler, speaker and speech coach

“Gerry has been a supplier of information as well as inspiration to many business owners the world over. The collection of touching stories in this book will demonstrate to you that he is a channel of positive influence in this world.”

– Robert D. Schofield, President,
Clarence Chamber of Commerce

“The secret behind great writing is to establish an emotional connection between the characters and the readers. This is a powerful connection that is brought to the forefront through wonderful tales of daily life.”

– Cliff Fazzolari, author of *Counting on a Miracle, In Real Life, Desperation, Waldorf & Juli, Eye in the Sky*, and *Money Changes Everything*

”My children lost their father at a young age, and my own father is soon to leave this earth, giving this collection of essays all the more poignancy for me. We are truly the products of our parents, as this inspiring collection demonstrates.”

– Michele Miller, Editor & Publisher,
Western New York Family Magazine

“This book will make you stop and think. *Our Fathers Who Art in Heaven* is a revelation that will fill your eyes with tears and your heart with laughter. In these days of overwhelming individualism, it’s a book to stop us in our tracks with our closest connection to ourselves! The tales will make your own life a story worth living better and, in the end, worth telling. This book is a tonic for our times. I can’t wait for *Our Mothers Who Art In Heaven*!

– Monsignor J. Patrick Keleher, Campus Minister,
State University of New York at Buffalo

The Vision

Our Fathers Who Art in Heaven is more than just a book; it's a cornerstone of a vision. Historically, society has given so much attention to the leadership and life lessons gleaned from corporate executives, politicians, historical figures, athletes, and entertainers, yet these famous people are very distant from everyday individuals. The purpose of this book is to allow ordinary people to share their "extra" ordinary experiences as they relate to their deceased father, whose energy continues to influence their daily lives and actions. Each of the 44 essays offers readers a candid peek at the family dynamic the author experienced, and identifies a principle of life and leadership, such as Attitude, Integrity, Determination, Compassion, Character, etc., essential to surviving in today's world of challenges. This insight and moving collection of short stories will motivate readers to discover hidden gems of leadership and wisdom in their own life.

About the Foundation

The proceeds from this book are going to the Our Fathers Who Art in Heaven Foundation (OFWAIHF – Section 501(c)(3) Non-profit Organization), a central source of inspiration for those who have lost their fathers or who are soon to be a father. Every year, beginning in 2005, the Foundation will hold Father's Day events to remember, share, and encourage others who have lost their father. Ultimately, the vision is for the Foundation to fund an Our Fathers Who Art in Heaven Hall of Fame. Those authors whose stories have been selected to appear in the book(s) will have the opportunity to showcase memorabilia from their father in an effort to inspire future fathers and leaders.

Those who make a donation of $50 or more to the OFWAIHF will receive a complimentary autographed copy of *Our Fathers Who Art in Heaven.*

To donate, make checks payable to OFWAIHF. We greatly appreciate your support and continued words of encouragement.

OFWAIHF
P.O. Box 502
Getzville, NY 14068

Dedication

To my father,
who taught me
to leave things better than I found them.

Acknowledgements xvii
Introduction xix

Attitude

"Ya Gotta Wanna"
By Gerry Murak 25

Integrity

Watermelon Memories
By Angie Klink 31

Ethical Training Begins at Home
By Pete Land 33

Looking Over My Shoulder
By Candy Killion 35

My Father's Promise
By Sal Amico M. Buttaci 37

A Giant Called Shorty
By David Thatcher 43

A Country Boy's Point of View
By T. Jackson Anderson 47

Memories

Dancing Lights, First Coffee
By Shelagh Wulff-Wisdom 51

Reel Event
By B.J. Taylor 55

Determination

The Fall Line
By Tom Pawlak 61

Grace
By Leanne Krause 65

The Art of Patience
By Linda E. Allen 67

Where There's a Will, There's a Way
By Renie (Szilak) Burghardt 71

Coming Up Roses
By Peri Shawn 75

Unspoken Lessons
By Patricia Asaad 79

Compassion

Mess Sergeant Muzzy, U.S.M.C.
By Thomas Edward 85

Peace for Pickles
By B.J. Taylor 89

The Faith of My Father
By Sharon Tabor Warren 93

The Lesson
By Jean Stewart 95

Treat Dad Like God This Father's Day
By Gregory J. Rummo 97

A Clacking Tongue
By Eileen Key 99

Wisdom

Just Four Words
By Mary Lou Healy....105

When In Doubt
By Anne Abernathy Roth....107

Patience by Example
By Sharon C. McGonigal.... 109

Don't Be Sorry
By Susan DeWolfe....113

Words of Wisdom
By Mike Marinaro....115

Inspiration

Where We Are
By Annie Shapero....119

Life Deals Some Bitter Pills
By Colleen Tillger.... 123

Gone But Not Forgotten… Love Lives On
By Kristy Gillinder.... 127

Old Spice
By Nancy Robinson.... 129

Character

The Day I Wasn't an All-Star
By Dan Markham....135

Consider and Respect Others First
By Patricia P. Miller....139

A Lesson on Success
By Gail Clanton Diggs 141

A Love Letter to My Dad on Father's Day
By Michele H. Lacina 145

My Greatest Teacher
By Margaret A. Elliott 147

What's In a Name?
By Vanessa Moore 149

Lessons from a Committed Father
By Barbara S. Greenstreet 151

Nature

The Fishing
By Gail Kavanagh 157

Family Trees
By Linda J. Parker 161

Of Men and Mountains
By Kristine Lowder 163

Inconsistencies
By Deborah Straw 171

Courage

Last Flight
By Dara Armstrong Lehner 177

My Own Unexpected Party
By Julie Atkin 179

Dinah Might
By Tom Basinski 181

Contributing Authors 185

About the OFWAIHF Founder and Creator
of the Who Art In Heaven™ Series 190

Submit Your Stories 191

Acknowledgements

Writing a book is not a simple task; it is a unique journey. You meet a lot of people along the way who become tremendous resources, and others who are advisors, mentors, and coaches. But before the journey even begins, you need a solid base to start with. That base for me is and has always been my family.

My wife, Barbara, has always been the biggest supporter of my dreams for the last thirty-five years. This book, and the goal of setting up the Our Fathers Who Art in Heaven Foundation, has been a dream for several years. When I finally made the commitment to the project, I quickly realized that this dream was bigger than I had imagined. In fact, at times this dream has been overwhelming; yet Barbara temporarily put aside her longtime art career to manage the ever-growing piles of paperwork that lay like snow blanketing every available counter space in our home. Barbara, "many thanks for all you do" are words that seem so deficient in expressing my gratitude. The many gentle nudges you have given me to keep me on track, even though we have never been on this journey before, have certainly demonstrated your love and devotion. I love you.

Thanks to our son, Andrew Murak, a graphic designer, who never complained about the many minor changes to the covers he designed for both the Sneak Preview and this inaugural volume, even after working ten-hour days at his "real" job. Even so, he never compromised his time or love for his wife and two sons. I marvel at your life balance and priorities.

To our daughter, Kimberly Murak, thank you for flying home, from the beautiful southwest, to become the "event planner and hands-on technician" for my first public speech about this book in June of 2004. I miss you so much, but I know you are living your dream. I am so proud of you. Your determination gives me courage to keep going.

To my mother, Gertrude Murak, whose words of encouragement always seemed to come at the right time during those phone calls I made when heading home at the end of my day. Thanks, Mom!

I am grateful to all of the writers from around the world who submitted their stories about their fathers for this first volume, and all of those who continue to send in their stories for future volumes. Thanks to each of you for opening your minds and hearts, and for sharing your candid creativity with the world.

My appreciation goes to the Independent Review Panel that had the seemingly impossible task of narrowing down the selections for this book. You made an overwhelming challenge possible.

To Sister Rose Mary Cauley and Patrick Welsh, two initial Board members. Your generosity and expertise in making the Our Fathers Who Art in Heaven Foundation a reality are greatly appreciated.

I would also like to thank Dawn and David Josephson of Cameo Publications, LLC for their guidance and direction. You are the patron saints of writers and publishers!

Two of my long-time co-workers and friends, Dave Paluch and Norm Preston, have been great influences on my life, more than they ever realized, and always had a joke or funny story, making sure I never took life too seriously. Unfortunately, neither will get to see this book; they both died last year, just a few months apart. It is so hard to believe they are gone. I will be sharing my stories of my experiences with them in my upcoming book *Our Friends Who Art in Heaven*. I miss you both.

To all my friends in the National Speakers Association, whose example and guidance convinced me that I could actually put together a book. Thank you for your support and words of encouragement that always seem to come at the perfect time.

I can't forget to say a few words about Peggy Murak, my Partner in my consulting practice, and Jill Walter, my Administrative Assistant and "Director of First Impressions," who both win the "survivor challenge" of sticking with me through this even when I tried to squeeze extra hours out of every day.

Finally, I would like to thank my deceased father. Whenever we would repair a vacuum cleaner in his basement workshop, he would put a sticker on the cleaner that carried his name, "Edward A. Murak." Dad, I never really knew how many lives you touched until your wake. Your inspiration will always live within me, and now, it will live in the hearts of others. Your "sticker" is now on this book, and your energy lives on!

Introduction

In 1995 I was traveling alone on a cross country flight. I was sitting in a window seat, and next to me was another weary traveler, sleeping soundly. Air travel has a way of pinning down type-A extroverts like me without batting an eyelash. I was trapped without anyone to talk to. At least I had a lot of time to think.

I already completed the paperwork I brought along. The flight was bumpy. The "Fasten Your Seatbelt" sign was glowing. My mind was wandering like a plane lost in the clouds. That's when the "BIG" question rolled between my ears: "What is the meaning of life?"

You are born, and before you know it, the mounds of daily challenges erase most of your early childhood memories. We quickly realize that we traveled at stealth speed from childhood thoughts of "there is nothing to do today" when our friends couldn't play, to today's thoughts of "what happened to the time?" I looked at my hands and realized the scars from childhood cuts were getting crowded out by wrinkles, and were marking time through any denial of aging. Then, I looked at the two wedding bands I wore, one on each hand. Yes, the two wedding bands often prompted puzzled glances from audience members when I gave a speech. "Why would you wear two wedding bands?" was the usual question.

As I gazed out the window, I quickly realized why the flight was so bumpy and why the "Fasten Your Seatbelt" sign was glowing above our heads—the dark and ominous storm clouds outside almost always assured a bumpy ride. On that particular flight, the cloud formations were beyond imagination. Any child's drawing would have been accurate. Every shape of cloud that one could possibly imagine seemed to show up for this storm. The pilot apologized for the bumpy ride, and said he would try to gain altitude and rise above the storm.

Little did the pilot realize he would also give rise to the purpose of this book. As the plane gained altitude, a beautiful blue sky began to peek through the dramatic cloud formations. Then, when the plane was above the clouds, the view was spectacular. The tops of the clouds, the billowing shapes, the shades of grey lit with accents of pure white, the shadows, and the piercing beams of light joined together to form an image worthy of the finest framed canvas in a prestigious gallery.

Then I started to think, why are the tops of clouds so beautiful? How many people, for how many thousands of years, could only see the bottoms of clouds or a partial side view when they gazed on a sunrise or sunset? Only for the last 100 of those tens of thousands of years could human beings see the tops of clouds. How privileged we are as a generation to be able to enjoy both walking through a forest and flying above the clouds. The master designer knew that some day people would come to enjoy the magnificent beauty of the top of a cloud!

So, we are born, we live, and then we die. As I sat in that airplane seat, I started to think about the millions of people who have passed from this earth. What do we know about them? I quickly realized that the best estate plan and will might leave financial continuity for the survivors, but what about the legacy of the person? What about the lessons of life and leadership they had experienced? The documented word, whether written or electronically recorded, is the only way we can be assured our thoughts will live way beyond our bodies.

"That is it!" I thought. "I need to write!" The only problem was that I could never figure out how to diagram a sentence in grammar school. I flunked English in college and had to take it in summer school. Whenever I have the occasion to use an easel in front of a live audience, I pray that someone would quickly invent a magic marker with a spell checker. But I needed to pass on the lessons I learned from my father, as well as the lessons I wanted to pass on to our daughter and son and their children. Then my inner dialogue changed: "Who said I can't write? I can think! I can use two fingers to type! I can write! I can write about why I wear two wedding bands!"

During the question and answer portion at the close of one of my speeches a few years earlier, a member of the audience asked, "Why do you wear two wedding bands?" My unrehearsed reply was, "Either I am very rich, very poor, or I am in trouble with two women or the law." And then I paused and raised my left hand to show the wide band whose crisp edges have long been worn smooth and I said, "This ring was given to me by my loving wife, Barbara, in 1970." Then I raised my right hand and I said, "This ring was given to me by my mother," and then I paused with a lump in my throat and a chill up my spine. Once I took a breath, I continued, "This ring was given to me by my mother after my father died in 1984. It was his 25th anniversary band, and I have worn it since he died."

As I started writing and rewriting the story about my father (See page 25) other events seem to coincidentally occur. The first was during a business trip to Chicago several years ago. I was standing in an executive's office, and I noticed an unusual photo on the file cabinet behind the desk. It was a photo of a man in what seemed to be a very old fashioned skiing gear. Out of curiosity I asked the executive if that was his father. He said it was. He then proceeded to tell me a very touching story about his deceased dad (See page 61). When he finished, I shared with him my story about my father and the significant impact he has had on all the work I have done, and in my commitment to leave things better than I find them. I also told him about this book. He asked if he could submit his story.

A couple of years later, I was heading home from a day of boating and stopped at a local gas station to fill up the tank in the boat. On the other side of the pump, a motorcyclist pulled up and got off the motorcycle to fill his tank. I smiled and said, "I wish my boat had your tank." He smiled and said he wished he had my boat. We laughed and then I noticed that his motorcycle had the most elaborate and unusual paint job on the tank and fenders; a Maltese cross, a Vargas girl, bullet holes, and other very unique details.

Having painted vehicles and motorcycles when I was a kid, I could appreciate that this was no ordinary paint job. I complimented him on the wonderful "art work" on two wheels. He said it was a tribute to his late father who recently passed away. I then told him that I had been working on a book for several years, more off than on, and it was about the lessons in life and leadership from deceased fathers. He smiled and turned toward his saddle bags, gently opened one of the flaps, and pulled out a couple pages of 8 ½ x 11 paper stapled together. He handed them to me and said, "Here, you can have this. It is a story about my late father who was a World War II pilot. The paint job on my motorcycle is the same as the paint job on the side of my father's plane. The only difference is that his bullet holes weren't painted on the plane. They were real!" (See page 181).

As I pulled away from the pumps and headed down the street, I looked in the rear view mirror to catch one more glimpse of that very special motorcycle. The moment my eyes moved from the road ahead to the mirror, the setting sun filled my mirror with the most brilliant light, and I could only hear the motorcycle pulling away.

When I reflect on those situations and others, I realize they were not "coincidences" at all; rather, total strangers (maybe even the spirits of all those deceased fathers) were guiding me to share these stories and the stories from 41 other individuals who were selected by an independent panel from over 120 submissions from over 6 countries. Even as I type this introduction we continue to get more inquiries and submissions. This book is in its final days before printing and Volume II is quickly becoming a reality.

So this book is the answer to the "BIG" question for me. These pages are devoted to fathers who have passed on lessons in life and leadership that many future generations can learn from for years to come. The bodies of these fathers have died, but their energy and spirit lives on.

"The reason a lot of people do not recognize opportunity is because it usually goes around wearing overalls looking like hard work."

– Thomas Edison

"Ya Gotta Wanna"

By Gerry Murak

Summer 1960. The hot and humid air hung on us like a wet t-shirt, but Dad wasn't going to let the summer heat stop us from completing our chores. We had a lot of gardening to do, and our goal was to get it all done that day.

As we worked, Dad thought it would help if we had an additional shovel, so he sent me next door to borrow a shovel from Mr. Kullen. I obliged, and that additional shovel helped us complete the job by late afternoon. Just as I was about to head over to Mr. Kullen's to return the shovel, Dad sternly said, "Don't return the shovel like that—clean it first!"

Dad wasn't someone you argued with. If he said do it, you did it. He stood over me in his dirty jeans and wiped the sweat from his brow. He was short and stocky but very solid. His gut was harder than the rocks that would occasionally block the path of our shovels.

I took the shovel to the edge of the yard and scraped off the clumps of dirt. Dad went back to his side of the yard and continued cleaning the lawn equipment. Satisfied that the shovel was clean, I headed over to Mr. Kullen's again.

"Gerald!" Dad yelled. He used my first name in full rather than simply calling me Gerry, so I knew what was coming next wasn't going to be good news. "Gerald! Where are you going with that shovel?" Before I could get a word out, the orders came down. "Get some coarse steel wool and clean the rest of the dirt off of that shovel!"

I knew there was no use talking back or consensus building, so I followed my orders. I went down into the cool basement workshop to get the steel wool. Before I could get back up the stairs, his voice filled the stairwell. "What's taking so long?" he asked.

"Coming, Dad." I hurried up the basement stairs, got outside, and polished the shovel.

Satisfied once again that the shovel was clean, I started back over toward Mr. Kullen's...again.

"Gerald! Where are you going with that shovel?"

By this time even a saint's patience would be in question. I mumbled under my breath: "Now what?"

"Oil that shovel!" Dad demanded.

"But Dad, we don't do that to our own shovels! Besides, it already looks better than when we borrowed it." Looking at Dad's face, I knew my comments didn't go over well.

"We will never have a problem if we want to borrow the shovel again," Dad said.

So, just as Dad had instructed, I oiled the shovel. It was at times like that when I had the feeling that I should have known what to do from the very beginning. I know Dad thought the extra effort should have been second nature to me.

I started working in my dad's business repairing vacuum cleaners when I was midway through grammar school. As I got older and worked other jobs, I always made time to help Dad in his business. Whether I worked as a burger flipper, a collision man, a shop teacher, a photographer, Director of Safety and Training, Packaging Manager or Production Manager, I worked in Dad's shop on nights and weekends. But it wasn't until a few years after Dad died that I realized the lesson of that shovel in my life: *Leave things better than you found them.*

But Dad's successful business had even greater significance. Dad wasn't born into wealth. The son of Polish immigrants, he was one of seven children growing up in Buffalo, NY. He left school in the sixth grade to peddle eggs on a bicycle. Every dollar he earned he turned in for the family. The six oldest children all left school and went to work so that the family would have enough money for the youngest to go to college. They didn't live through the depression—they worked through it!

In those days, there were no convenience foods or mega super stores. When Dad was growing up, he bought food at the farmer's market. When the family had a few extra coins, they would buy a duck. They wasted nothing. Charnina, or duck's blood soup, was a specialty. As kids, they took turns with the chore of draining the duck's blood. Today, kids groan about taking out the garbage—ah, the "good old days"!

Jobs were scarce, so as a young man Dad went to work on the Tennessee Valley Authority project at a CCC (Civilian Conservation Corps) camp. He experienced tragedy at an early age when the camp barracks burned to the ground, and he lost many friends.

A few years later he returned to Buffalo and met Mother at St. Rita's lawn fete. WWII broke out, and Dad wasn't eligible for the war, so he worked at an aircraft plant and then a steel mill. After the war, he sold vacuum cleaners door to door. By the time I was nine, I worked in my Dad's shop in the basement, hand polishing vacuum cleaner parts with steel wool.

Realize that this was not a shop out of a catalog with pegboard and fancy hooks. The shop area was cramped into an 8' x 8' space. Dad stored his tools in old bent up metal ice cube trays and cake pans. Nails served as hooks for a few tools he used a lot. His stool had an old rug folded over the seat for padding. He used every available space, even the above-head floor joists had vacuum parts hanging from nails.

To say that Dad was frugal and hard working is an understatement. As a result of his discipline, he was very successful as a vacuum cleaner salesman, regularly winning national sales contests and receiving prizes such as wristwatches, clothing and even vacation trips. By 1950, he had saved enough money to have a house built, and he paid for it in cash. Well, not all of it. The builder didn't follow my dad's specifications, so my Father did not pay for the house in full. The builder took Dad to court. He represented himself before the judge and won the case. He always stood up for what was right.

But Dad's success never meant a free ticket for me or my two brothers and sister. Allowances were unheard of. If you wanted something for yourself, you earned it by working—cutting lawns, painting houses, babysitting, etc. For me, it was repairing vacuum cleaners. My two brothers and sister never worked in the shop. It was just my father and me.

I worked in Dad's shop for over 30 years, regardless of my day job. If I didn't have spare time, I made time, until the day he died. I was there so often that I knew every inch of space, every part, every tool, every two-by-four, and every floor joist above my head where we would hang various parts from large nails.

Several years after my father passed, Mom decided to sell the house and move into an apartment. We gave away a lot of memories. Weeks later, when the house was empty, I took one final walk through the dream Dad worked so hard to build from very meager beginnings.

The hardest part was my last visit to the cool basement. Tucked into one corner was the 8' x 8' shop. It was barren now except for the nails protruding from the two-by-fours and floor joists. I stood in the center of all that emptiness and felt a fullness in my chest welling up. As I looked around, I reflected on all the things I learned in that basement. The one lesson that stood out was the dignity of working with your hands and getting dirty. Back then I regretted working while my school friends would be out playing, but I don't regret it now because that is how I came to know my father.

As I gazed up and stared at the floor joists above me—where for days before I had pulled all of the parts off of the nails, I found a lapel pin stuck into one of the floor joists. I never saw this pin before in all the hours I spent in the shop taking parts off the nails. I couldn't make out what the pin said, so I reached up and pulled it down and dusted it off.

The pin had three simple words on it: "Ya Gotta Wanna." At that moment, it all made sense. Everything my father had ever taught me was summed up in those three words.

Take a lesson from my father. There is nothing anyone can do to help you overcome the hardships and challenges in your life, *"Ya Gotta Wanna."*

Edward A. Murak died June 19, 1984

"Honesty is the first chapter in the book of wisdom."

– Thomas Jefferson

Watermelon Memories

By Angie Klink

Often as a child I complacently thought my quiet father was paying absolutely no attention to my behavior or my comings and goings. It seemed Daddy left the bulk of parenting to my mother. Yet if my actions became less than forthright, he would abruptly appear in my radar and take me to task to jolt me onto the path of good manners and rightful living. Take, for instance, a feverishly hot August day when I was 10. I was playing outside with my best friend Brenda. I wanted the cold, crisp watermelon I knew was in our refrigerator. But I didn't want Brenda to have a single taste of our precious watermelon.

Brenda and I were swinging on my backyard swing set constructed of plumbing pipes—the old-fashioned metal kind of pipes, not plastic. In fact, now that I think about it, the pipes were made of lead and painted with layer-upon-layer of dangerous lead paint that we didn't know we should fear in the 1960s.

Anyway, answering the call of the watermelon, I ran inside the house as Brenda glided on the swing waiting for me to return. (I think I told her I had to go to the bathroom.) I hurried to the kitchen before Brenda missed me for too long, flung open the refrigerator door and reached in to take a quick bite of juicy, pre-cut melon with plans to run immediately back outside, tummy full, thirst quenched. But my father entered just in time to see me ravenously chomp into a liquid, pink slice and push the remainder into the fridge.

"Hey, you take a piece out to your friend," Daddy said. He scowled and his tone was gruff.

Surprised and embarrassed, caught in my self-centered act, I balked and hem hawed. It would be too much of a hassle to carry the drippy fruit to Brenda. But Daddy shoved a watermelon slice in my hand and commanded me out the back door with the order to "be hospitable to a guest."

Guest? It was just Brenda. She lived next door.

I was miffed but did as I was told. I loved watermelon, and I wanted all of the crimson lusciousness to myself. I didn't want to *waste* it on a friend. Daddy read my intentions well when he witnessed my glutinous performance at the harvest gold Kenmore. He wasn't about to let me get away with being selfish.

It's funny—I think of that fleeting watermelon moment often (especially when I eat the delectable fruit). Yet, if my father were living today (he's been gone since 1987), I'm guessing he would have no recollection of our melon standoff. A seemingly mundane event of childhood can become a lesson that sticks around for the long haul, but a parent spouts so many instructions and bits of advice in a day's time, it's hard to know which words will soak in to a child's core. (I wonder what life tutorials I'm unknowingly recording on my sons' memory ledgers.)

Brief, simple moments of parental guidance whittle a child's character ever so slightly towards its final mold. My father's upstanding ways, his steady integrity and unwavering principles simmered beneath each of his well-timed nudges of instruction that prodded me in the right direction throughout my growing years.

Daddy's unyielding how-to-treat-a-friend commando that summer day when I was 10 became a recorded tape that has hummed in my head for over 35 years. Its underlying message still comes through loud and clear and will forever hold validity:

Share your watermelon, Angie. A friend is waiting. Hoarding the goodness of life is a lonely way to live.

Ethical Training Begins at Home

By Pete Land

My father, Bill Land, was born in Norfolk, Virginia in 1905. His father owned a real estate company. When my dad was six years old, his father, W.H. Land, was inspecting some industrial property and fell to his death from a train trestle. In 1932 my parents moved to Wilmington, North Carolina with my brother, sister, and me.

One of the most memorable characteristics about my father was his unwavering honesty and integrity. If I did something I shouldn't have done… or didn't do something I should have done, my dad would ask, "Pete, what happened?" I realize now what an astute question that was. It is non-judgmental and non-accusatory. It's a neutral, fact-finding question.

On the occasions when I would be honest and confess my sins he would say, "Son, I am proud of you for telling the truth. Go to your room and think about what you have learned about this situation. Come back in an hour and share with me what you have learned." His strategy tended to motivate me to tell the truth, despite how embarrassing.

However, on a few occasions I tried to weasel, waffle, and quibble to the point that I told a lie. When the truth was finally known, this is what happened: I had to go to a bush in our back yard, cut a switch (and it better not be too small) and give it to my dad. Before he administered a little corporal punishment he would always say, "Son, misbehaving is part of being a little boy, but lying is unacceptable at any age." It was a lifelong lesson in integrity.

When I was twelve, I asked, "Dad, what do you think I should be when I grow up?"

He replied, "Son, I don't really care what profession you choose for your life's work; but, whatever you choose to be, be a good one! In this country, we honor excellence. It doesn't matter what profession you pursue, but I want you to become as good at that job as you possibly can." Then he smiled and said with a twinkle in his eye, "I don't care if you chose to be a bank robber—just be America's greatest bank robber," and he hugged me.

Finally, one Monday I asked my dad if I could borrow five dollars. He asked, "What for?"

I don't recall the reason now; it was not important. But he said, "Son, I will loan you five dollars today. When can I expect you to repay me?"

After pondering how many lawns I could cut in the next few afternoons, I said, "I will pay you back next Friday afternoon."

He said, "Fine, Son, here's five dollars." Throughout the remainder of the week he never mentioned the loan or reminded me of the due date.

I really had to scramble and cut lawns every afternoon to earn that money by Friday. In the mid-1940s the going rate for cutting a lawn in our neighborhood was about one dollar. After dinner on Friday I went to my room, gathered up a disorderly handful of dollar bills and coins, counted them to be sure it was exactly five dollars in U.S. currency, went downstairs, and ceremoniously counted the loot out to my dad.

He said, "Thank you, Pete" and put the money in his pocket. As I turned to walk away, he called, "Wait, Son, come back." He took out his wallet, removed a crisp new five dollar bill, gave it to me, and said, "It's worth five dollars to me to see you learning to be reliable and to honor your commitments. This five dollar bill is yours."

Those five dollars were priceless in my development.

My father died at eighty-six years of age from complications of diabetes. In all the years I knew him, I never saw him do or say anything that was not the absolute truth as he knew it. Yes, he lived the values he tried to teach me.

Thanks, Dad.

Looking Over My Shoulder

By Candy Killion

The Sixties was a turbulent time, no matter which generation you happened to belong to. Images of Vietnam burst onto our TV screens at dinner time, and anyone over thirty mostly shook their heads at the sight of the unwashed, ragged young growing hair-to-there, sitting out and sitting-in, in protest. I was a teenager then with flowers in my hair, urging my widower father to stop buying plastic wrap at the grocery store, because that company made napalm.

It was one of the few, subtle antiwar gestures he could swallow. Dad had served in the Po Valley with the 10th Mountain, in another time. While the Hawks and the Doves went round on whether this time was a war or a conflict, my father's take on our involvement was simple. The young men who were 1-A were simply doing their jobs, now as when he was young. For my father, there were few grey areas on the topic of taking responsibility. You either did the right thing, or you didn't.

That isn't to say that my father wore blinders, that he held a myopic view of the world. It was not his way or the highway. Rather, Dad enjoyed a good verbal joust, and as the father of daughters—and having raised them singly, to boot—he was always challenging us to convince him:

"Tell me why you think your stand is right. Then, by God, live it!"

At fifteen, I was outspoken in my condemnation of the war. I sat on the sidewalk downtown, holding my flower-powered placard, urging anyone who would listen to speak up so the growing number of neighborhood guys I'd gone to school with would come home. I didn't throw bottles at the cops, spit at passers-by, or ever even remotely come close to being arrested. I used words, and only words.

One day, my father plunked down his coffee cup at the kitchen table and surveyed me, arranging my parted-down-the-middle hair in the hall mirror. I'd just come back from another rally.

"How's the cause?"

"It got a little hairy down there. There was a group that was just—I don't know. Out of control. They looked high." I bit my lip, and continued brushing my hair. Dad didn't say a word. He waited for what came next.

"And," I looked ahead, meeting my father's eyes in the mirror, "it came to me. Suddenly, I felt like I was in the wrong place. These people were not serious about the cause. Dad, it was an excuse for a party! Suddenly, I felt like I was sitting in the middle of a field of sheep."

My father smiled, just a little. "And?"

I turned to look at him. "And I thought about you standing over my shoulder. My stomach twisted. I believe in what I am saying, but surrounding myself with people whose tactics are iffy—well, Dad, it just didn't feel right. Irresponsible, even. There has to be a better way."

My father lay a hand on my shoulder. "And, you will find it."

It has been over three decades since that conversation in front of the mirror, and my father has been gone nearly as long. I am the older generation now, my own children grown and gone and the next sprouting up strong and tall behind them. And there has hardly been a day since that I've not stepped in front of my mirror, in the midst of one of my life's small or serious decisions, mulling over the direction of the action and inactions that make up a life, and thought about him.

He still stands in the mirror behind me, nodding in assent when the right thing is to be done. That is his gift, and his legacy to me.

My Father's Promise

By Sal Amico M. Buttaci

My father built his good reputation on the bedrock of his word. What he promised, he delivered. He never cared if others found his ways dumb-fashioned. Even words spoken in anger or in the humor of the moment, promises no one in his right mind would expect Papa to keep, he kept.

"I gave my word," he'd say in his defense. "My word is good."

Though a man of short stature—he was only 5'5"—my father held his head up, walked taller than all the heroes of my younger days. He'd say to us, "I can look in the mirror eye to eye with myself and never turn away in shame or guilt. A man, who promises one thing, does another: What do you think? Is he the kind of man you would trust?"

Papa immigrated to America from Sicily in 1920 when he was only fifteen years old. He had spent two years in a Catholic seminary where he enjoyed studying Latin and Literature, but one day his widowed mother ordered him back to their little mountain village of Acquaviva Platani, for she had decided to leave half her children and rejoin the other half, all of whom lived in New York. We always referred to this dual family of ours as "the Sicilian Sicilians in Sicily" and "the American Sicilians in America." Our uncle and aunts, Ziu Vanuzzu, Za Serafina, and Za Ninetta lived in Sicily. Uncle Joe, Uncle Paul, and Aunt Laura lived in New York. My father, who was the youngest of Grandma's children, all the adults, including my mother, called him "Michelino"—little Michael.

Papa was a man who valued the ideals he learned as a child. He was always respectful towards everyone with whom he came in contact. No one was beneath or above him. "Maybe in Sicily, but not here," he would say. "In America, everybody is equal!" Still, he distrusted anyone who wasn't Sicilian like him, which meant the "Americani," a catchword for non-Sicilians. He'd reprimand us with "Where did you learn that? From the Americani?" Or "We don't forget to use manners around here, do we? What are we, Siciliani or Americani?" Or "You're ashamed to kiss your father? How wonderful! And did you learn that from the Americani who would sell their parents for a few dollars?"

Yes, it was difficult being the son of an immigrant father and a mother who, though born on the Lower Eastside of New York in 1913, might just as well have been an immigrant. Her mother took her back to Acquaviva Platani when she was only three months old! Both my parents spoke with accents, especially my mother, whom I tried to hide from my friends because their mothers were mostly Irish who spoke English with their cute Irish brogues. The fact that she was the kind of mother so many of these same friends wished they had did not matter to that young boy I was. Mama had an unshakable faith in God and in my father. For their children they would have gone without shoes and bread: I know this now without a doubt but in those early days of mine, what did I understand about values and sacrifice and the blessings of having parents like them!

My father never broke his word. He never talked merely to hear himself speak. He never lied, even when lying would've seemed the wiser thing to do. He usually did not even resort to being tactful. He said it "like it was" and if that displeased or upset someone, too bad! "I got to live with myself first," Papa argued. "If I have to start hating myself because what I say is a lie, what kind of a man am I?"

On more than one occasion, my father would tell the story we called "Papa's Lucky Friend." When I first heard him tell it, I couldn't believe such a thing could happen. I couldn't believe my father with all his intelligence and common sense could actually do what he did way back in 1928. And when he'd begin the story in the company of my visiting friends, I would try hard to round up my pals and head us all towards the door. But they loved my father's stories and would insist on hearing this one too.

Papa would begin with "Back in 1928, I saved some money and bought myself a Ford." The larger the audience the better. We could tell by his eyes—dark brown and twinkling—that he just loved telling the "Papa's Lucky Friend" story. He'd gesture with his arms, raise and lower his voice at the best parts. He'd pause for effect. Speak in his own voice, then in the voice of his "lucky friend." Papa would recount the story the way I'd imagine Nobel Prize winners might proudly narrate the achievements that earned them acclaim; however, Papa would do so with little modesty. After all, the point of the story demonstrated my father's adherence to principle. It spoke in his behalf and he himself felt proud and deserving of the praise he expected at the end of his story.

Papa continued. "I loved that car! I'd take my friend Joe with me for rides down streets in New York and even New Jersey when most streets weren't streets but dusty dirt roads and not too many houses on each side. Anyway, I loved that car. Proud, you know? I mean times were good, but not that good that everybody could run out and buy himself a new car."

"So what happened next?" my sister would ask. And Papa would raise his hand to mean "Wait. I'm coming to it." And he'd keep his hand up till the room quieted down and he had all of our attentions again. When he dropped his hand, he raised the other and pointed at the imaginary car at his side. "Beautiful it was, but you know sometimes a thing is beautiful but has no brains. All show. No action."

We would look at one another, those who'd heard this story before and those who were hearing it for the first time. No one told a tale like Papa! He'd make you wait all right. He knew just what to say and when to say it. We waited till he was good and ready when at last he'd go on. "The damn thing stalled."

"The new car?" asked Anna. "Out of gas?" my friend Alfred offered. "What happened, Pa?" I asked, practically on cue.

"I will tell you what happened," said Papa. "I was mad, real mad with that car. It had stalled like that a couple times when I drove it by myself, but now it was making me look bad in front of Joe. I let out a few curse words." Mama shook her head, but she was smiling. "I won't repeat them here," he said, chuckling.

"Anybody want some soda?" Papa asked the crowd that day. That old ploy we knew so well. Oh Pa, with a little education you could've been a great public speaker. You surely knew how to grab your listeners, hold them, shake them, and let them go in your good time. "Peppina," he'd say to Mama, "Any more orange soda?" and Mama would check the refrigerator, bring a bottle back to the table, and Papa would pour the glasses we held to the tilted bottle.

"The car stalled. Did I say that already? Oh yeah, that damn car stalled. So what now? Remember I am mad. The car is not working so good, but the car is also making me look like a man who bought a lemon at the car lot. I turned to my friend Joe and I say, 'Joe, this damn car stalls one more time and it's yours.' Well, Joe, he laughs like a crazy guy. 'It's mine?' Joe says. Then he laughs all over again. 'Stalls again and the car belongs to me? Come on, Mike. You can't be serious,'" said Papa's American co-worker (or he would've called him "Michelino").

"Poor Joe. Laughing like a crazy guy and thinking I'm the crazy one because of what I said when the car stalled on me. I didn't say anything. I knew I was serious. I just prayed the car wouldn't stall again because I had made a promise when I was mad. Those words flew out of my mouth. My words. A promise to my friend."

"So the car gets started after some time fooling around with it, and we are on our way down the dirt roads again. Joe and me, we're laughing like schoolboys. What a car! Brand new and acting like a loser. We laughed about how it suddenly had gone dead on us."

"End of story?" asked Alfred. We all shook our heads. "There's more," I said.

Papa poured some orange soda for himself and we waited patiently as he downed the whole glass in one lift of the glass. "Not the end yet," he said to Alfred. "But almost. Well, everything's going good until—*poof*! The damn car starts making a funny coughing sound and once again we are sitting inside a deadbeat. Of course, Joe thinks this is very funny. Again with the laughing. He's laughing so loud I think maybe he's gonna pass out from laughing. 'Hey, Mike, some car, huh? It stalled again. Why don't we get out and push it off the road. Get some mechanic to look at it. Whatta you say, Mike?' Then Joe goes back to laughing his head off."

Papa decided to stand up and move his arms back in a favorite stretch of his. No one said a word. It was obvious the story wasn't over yet. We all waited for Papa to sit down again. He put his head down and moved an imaginary something on the tablecloth. When he lifted his head again, he had the look of a man with a ready punch line. "I got out of the car and slammed the door. I walked around to the other side where Joe was sitting there still laughing. I tapped on his window and he cranked it down. 'Here, Joe,' I said. 'It's yours.'

'The key is mine?' he asked. 'What you want me to do with it?'

'It goes with the car,' I said. 'The key, the car—they're yours.' And with that I start walking down the dirt road, on my way home."

At that point I asked the same question I always asked Papa at the end of the "Papa's Lucky Friend" story. "Wasn't that a dumb thing to do, Pa?"

And as always, he would stare at me, long and hard, with his dark eyes misting. "Sure. A very dumb thing. Tell me something. Am I dumb?"

"Oh no, Pa!" "Oh no, Mr. Buttaci!" We were all quick to make the point perfectly clear. Still, it sounded like a very dumb thing to do. And Papa did it.

"This is the lesson time now," Papa said in closing. "Never make promises you can't keep. Never swear you're gonna do this or that without thinking about it first. Don't give your word when you're mad or tired or not sure. Find the best time to make promises, understand? Why do I say that?" He didn't wait for an answer. "Because a good person never promises what can't be delivered. If you say it, you do it. Even if it's dumb, you gotta see it through. Was I dumb?" Papa held up his "stop" hand and confessed, "Giving that car was the dumbest thing I ever did. Now the world will say I was dumb because the world has a pretty good idea new cars don't come easy so they shouldn't go easy either. The world figures it all out in dollars. What does the thing cost? And the world might say that my car was worth more than that dumb stupid promise I made in a moment of anger, but I don't agree with the world, ok? I say the promise—my word I gave Joe—yes! That promise out of this mouth was everything!"

I don't know how many times I heard Papa tell that story. He told it often and after each time I couldn't bring myself to comprehend how a few words could be worth more than a shiny new Ford. But my father did, and so did I once I became a man anxious to become so much like him that there are times I tell stories of my own, stories in which I am not the hero, but the fool doing something I promised, even when the outcome worked against me.

There are times when I think about my father, gone since 1987, and wish God would grant me a few minutes of his company. I'd tell him how right he was. How the lessons he taught about being honest, responsible, even noble, were lessons not really wasted on me at all. Sometimes I speak his same words, feel my own dark eyes mist in the name of sensitivity, and feel the same pride he felt when he did the right thing, regardless of how the world might have judged him.

So all these years I've tried my best to walk as straight as he, to never forget promises are more than words one simply gives away. Like my father who built "cathedrals" with the honesty of his words, I smooth the mortar of my own words between the crevices stone to build spires tall enough to scrape the floor of Heaven.

A Giant Called Shorty

By David Thatcher

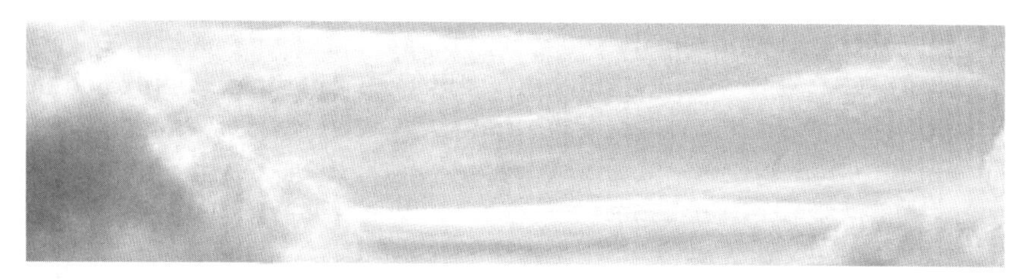

His name was Arthur, but I never heard anyone call him that. All adults in my little world knew him as "Shorty." That's because in Dad's youth, growing up a stepchild on an Indian reservation, he'd often run away to join traveling carnivals with his older brother. In carnivals every one had a nickname and Uncle Alton being taller, was called "Stretch." Some Sheriff would invariably catch the wandering boys and a telegram would be sent. Their stone-faced Indian stepfather would eventually arrive to take them back home. He'd sit there wearing a dark suit and kneading the brim of his hat in whatever jail they were in, until the prodigals were brought forth. It is likely that little conversation passed among them on the train ride home; both boys had told him often enough already that they hated him. He would take them home, so they could run away again.

When I met Arthur, he was 43 and I was one day old. He was a man with many talents and even more gentle tricks. He would often say, "Davey, it was a rough day at work, it'd do me some good, if you'd just read to me a little while. Would you get a book you like, and read some for me Son?"

I remember being in a doctor's waiting room as my little brother got his shots. I showed my dad an ad for *Encyclopedia Britannica*, and asked him for those books. I don't know how, but he bought those books for me. I probably would not be an engineer today, if he had not. A 1964 edition of *Encyclopedia Britannica* is one of my dearest possessions. I wish I could hug him now, and thank him for the encyclopedias.

Four decades removed from those moments, my heart still aches for the graceful subterfuge in the man. If I asked him a question, and he did not know the answer, he would make up something. I know that now; but back then I would have fought the biggest boy in the third grade if he said my dad was wrong.

It would be so wonderful to go to him for advice when I have personality conflicts at work. No doubt he would listen patiently as I explained in excruciating detail how I was right and everyone else was wrong. Then he would probably gently suggest "Now Davey, you know how you get sometimes." Part of the sadness in death is that it leaves the living only daydreams and memories.

Once I dragged a half-dead stray puppy home. Dad helped me care for it until it ignored our efforts and became fully dead. I ran out of the house crying and threw myself on a pile of sand that he had hauled in to re-do the driveway. Arthur came out there and just sat listening to me sob for a long time. Then he began wondering out loud what heaven might be like. I am sure he said some things far outside theological conventional wisdom. As he spun his tales of the afterlife, I slowly turned over, wiping sand and tears from my face. I nestled close to him and listened. He told me that no person or animal that has ever been truly loved could ever be truly dead. Dad helped me believe that in some place beyond our Earthly grasp, we will all be together again someday.

Arthur was easy to be with, in a way that is hard to define. He could see humor in nearly anything. Added to that, there was an infectious confidence that seemed to swirl about him. This trait was most clearly seen in his work away from work. After he came home from the aircraft factory, Dad worked on sick bicycles, televisions, lawn mowers, air conditioners, cars, and many other things. He was the neighborhood fix-it man. In the ten years I was lucky enough to be with Dad, I saw him repair some things he would have been hard pressed to identify. In retrospect, I can only surmise that Arthur was not the type to let seemingly complex things get the best of him.

There was the time a truck hit a telephone pole. It destroyed a transformer, causing a power surge that wrecked a neighbor's television. Dad fixed the TV on their promise of payment once insurance paid. Well, the neighbors got the check but never paid, and that caused a little friction at my house. Mom always had a talent for stating her opinion in ways that left a lasting impression. It's a very clear memory for me, peeking around the kitchen doorway as my mother tried to have an argument with Arthur.

She was saying, "I can't believe the way you let people walk all over you, Shorty. They owe us money, aren't you gonna do anything about it?" He smiled and said, "Honey, it's just a few dollars. The worst thing you can do to some people is let 'em keep being just like they are." Of itself that is a valuable thing to know: in the long run, nobody really ever gets away with anything. My father was wise enough to know a few dollars were not worth argument, understanding that outlook pushes outcome for all of us, and no debts go unsettled.

Some early Saturday mornings I would sit in his lap, eating dry Cheerios from a lime green bowl, watching Laurel and Hardy. We were the only ones awake in the house. I would sit there with his arms around me, spitting cereal all over the coffee table during the best parts. Arthur would tell me about times and places I did not understand back then. He talked about carnivals and reservations, and a sad quiet man in a dark suit. He told me sometimes he wished he could apologize and that he "just did not know back then." I wish now I had asked him if that was why he was so careful with people's feelings. Most likely I only asked him if the carnival had elephants.

The greatest lessons my dad ever taught me? I am fairly sure he did not know I was listening closely, as we watched Stan and Ollie together. Reservations and carnivals just swirled around inside my head back then, but I came to sort it all out and learn something. I learned that I should be very careful how I deal with each person in my life. Without knowing, I could be saying or doing things at any moment that will ache in my heart for decades to come. When or if that should occur, I might have no one to hear my regrets, except a fat kid with a mouthful of Cheerios.

A Country Boy's Point of View

By T. Jackson Anderson

Many people have asked me where I get my occasionally unique perspective on things. They usually say those "stupid ideas" or "outdated notions" but I know they are kidding and really mean unique perspective. The best way to explain my values would be, I suppose, to start at the beginning. An obvious starting point but a good one nonetheless. I was born in Clearwater, Florida. My father, along with my grandfather and another man, owned a traveling carnival so by the time I was five years old, I had been in thirty some odd states. When I turned six and had to start school, my father sold his share and we moved to Lincoln, Alabama. Lincoln, at the time, was a small town about ten miles east of Talladega.

My first introduction to the free enterprise system came not too long after our move to Lincoln. After our move, my dad worked for a lumber and trucking company hauling wood cores to the paper mill. One evening he drove his truck into our yard and unloaded a huge bundle of one inch square wooden slats, each of which was about fifteen feet long. My dad told me that in the pile of wood lay the new bicycle for which I had been asking. Naturally, at six I didn't understand this was figurative and eagerly began moving slats looking for a new Schwinn. Fortunately, before any major splinters were acquired, my dad explained to me that the means to obtain the bike lay there, not the actual bike. He said, "Anything worth the having is worth the earning."

Let me explain; in the rural area where we lived, everyone gardened on a large scale. One of the staples in every garden was tomatoes. Tomato plants needed stakes for support when the fruit started "makin." All I had to do was take the handsaw and cut the slats into six foot lengths, bundle them in tens with twine, make a couple of poster board signs and wait. So I did. At the end of the summer I had amassed a fortune to rival Bill Gates, or, in other words, $300.00. My dad, having taught me the lesson he wanted, bought me the bike. He then took me to our local bank and let me open a savings account, telling the teller, "A working man's got to put some aside when he can."

I learned most of the big lessons in life from my dad, usually just by watching. I can still remember him coming home and working in our garden until well after dark, even though he had been up at 4 a.m. to deliver a load of cores. Of course, the payoff for all his hard work was a full freezer and pantry, not to mention the bounty on the supper table every night. My dad made me finish a season of little league one summer because, as he said, "You don't have to do it again, but once you start something, you finish it. Don't make commitments lightly, son, and you won't have the need to quit half done."

As I got older, like most fathers and sons, my dad and I argued about everything. I was young, idealistic, embracing the notion of life, liberty, and most importantly, the pursuit of happiness. My interpretation and Dad's differed quite a bit. My view had nothing of the responsibility that goes along with freedom that my dad seemed to believe was so important. Now that I am older, I can see that he was right. The Constitution doesn't guarantee the right to stay out past midnight on a school night.

Most of the views I have spring from the rural traditions by which my dad raised me. They are not so different, I believe, even now, in any rural community. The notions that hard work, honesty, and a little prayer to a god who helps those who help themselves will make everything come out all right. These are the values I learned going to Sunday school, the sale barn, the feed shop and the coffee shop with my dad. My dad was seventy-seven years old when he died and his beliefs served him for all those years. Those are the beliefs which serve me today. I may be a little hick and a dab naïve, but I believe that nothing of value is free; it is better to tell the truth and get it over with; and a working man has to put a little something away when he can. Of course, that is just this country boy's point of view.

"When drinking water, remember its source."

– Chinese proverb

Dancing Lights, First Coffee

By Shelagh Wulff-Wisdom

With a finger raised to pursed lips, my father appeared in the doorway of my bedroom and whispered, "Come with me." Without hesitation, I put down my book, pushed back the warm comforter on my bed, and tiptoed down the hall behind his looming figure. We stopped in the softly-lit kitchen, and he handed me his heavy sheepskin coat. There was no urgency in his voice or actions as he pointed, smiling, to the front door. I sensed an impending adventure as I looked into his face and saw the sparkle in his eyes.

His coat was heavy and smelled of hay, cows, and Old Spice. I stuffed the legs of my cotton pajama bottoms into the top of my boots, and slipped out onto the porch where he waited patiently. A faint yellow glow from the small kitchen light beamed softly through the window onto the steps. The night was cold, still, and damp. The moon hung precariously in a deep indigo sky, and stars twinkled and blinked brightly. It was a week away from Christmas. I was sixteen years old.

The vinyl seat of the pickup was cold, and the instrument panel threw an eerie orange glow on our faces as Dad turned the ignition key. He rolled the truck down the hill and drove slowly to the cattle guard, crossing it before turning on the headlights. Slowly we drove toward town and up the hill next to the highway. From there, one could see the sleeping town below, nestled next to the rambling Platte River. He parked the truck facing the north, and left it running to warm the crisp December night.

It was eleven o'clock, and the streets of the town below were void of traffic, save for the occasional vehicle. Lights twinkled and sparkled everywhere in anticipation of the upcoming holidays. The residents that lived next to the old high school on the hill at the east end of town had placed red, white and yellow Christmas lights on the huge pine tree in their yard. A dominant display on the highest point in town, the tree could be seen from miles around. Throughout the quiet streets, running lights raced around housetop and porch railings, bright colors peeked through branches, bushes and windows. Santa and his eight reindeer arched over the courthouse, gleaming faintly. The lights sparkled and glittered, and I felt so special sitting in the truck with my father, watching the blinking lights below.

Then, with a drawn breath and widened eyes, I suddenly realized why we sat in that old truck on the hill, late at night with everyone else tucked in their beds. It had nothing to do with Christmas or the glinting, racing lights of town, for they were small tokens compared to the spectacle that beamed and pulsated far to the north on the distant, unreachable horizon. Strobes of brilliant hazy blues, pinks, violets, yellows and reds stretched and pulsated across the purple skies to the north. Stars blinked in their midst, dowdy compared to the radiant beams as they flashed and blended into one another.

"Dancing lights." My father breathed huskily, "Those are dancing lights." I looked at him and was suddenly struck by the importance of this time; me and my dad stealing away in the dark of night to watch the dancing lights. He turned to me and asked, "Do you know what else they're called?"

"The northern lights," I answered. "Aurora borealis. We studied it in science." I gazed through the warming windshield pitted with rock nicks spider webbing through the glass. I was reluctant to even blink for fear of missing one splendid flash of vivid color as it swept across the horizon. We watched in silence for a few moments, and then I questioned my father about the "dancing lights."

"Oh, that's just what my dad called them," he said simply. He took a deep breath, and without looking, he reached to his worn thermos bottle lying on the seat. His eyes never left the light show in the sky as he slowly unscrewed the top of the thermos and poured steaming coffee in the stainless steel cup. He took a small sip, and then looked toward me, offering me the cup.

I reached for the cup, wondering if he knew I'd never tasted coffee. I knew it smelled warm and rich, but I'd never cared to try it. Somehow, tonight, I felt all grown up. Touching the cup to my lips, I took a tiny, hesitant sip. It was very warm—not too hot. It tasted brown, mellow. I took a bigger swallow and passed the cup back, feeling the steamy brew as it found it way down to my stomach. I settled deeper into my father's coat and the seat of the pickup. We sat riveted to the phenomenal marvel that nature had provided. The dancing lights performed; they waltzed, pirouetted, dipped, dived, and fanned across the dark sky backdrop.

"Dad, can you dance?" I asked. His laughter. "No. And I can't swim either." He looked sideways at me, grinning broadly. "Your mother can dance, though. She loves to dance. She can't swim either. But you—you're lucky. You can dance and swim both." His right hand went to his shirt pocket where he ferreted out his cigarettes and matches. I secretly feared he would offer me one. The flame from the struck match turned his face blue for an instant, then orange as he lit his cigarette. He cracked the window down to let the smoke escape, and it furled lazily into the December night.

Minutes ticked away as we passed the steel cup between us, enjoying the quiet, relishing the serenity and the gift that graced that moment in time. There was more present than blood, a family name, and sharing coffee. In that concrete moment of the magical season, our names were etched together in the sky and a memory was engraved forever on our hearts. We watched our kaleidoscope of pulsing beams sway, jump and flash. A shooting star drew our eyes for one fleeting moment to the west, but it, too, seemed faded compared to the dancing lights.

When the coffee was gone, we began to talk. We talked about the horses, cows, sheep and school. We talked about my plans after graduation and about two horses I was training. We discussed friends from school, what to get everyone for Christmas, planting another windbreak in the spring, winter wheat, and names for the foals that would be born in May. That night my father told me how he homesteaded on Lightning Creek and about a bay mare he called "Babe." He told me about his first team of horses and how he was the pitcher for the champion softball team. He talked about his brothers and his parents, and how they'd come from Germany. He asked me questions about piano lessons and high school rodeo, and what my favorite color of horse was.

We talked until the dancing lights began to fade. When a small group of deer passed in front of the pickup just a few feet away, the poignant spell was broken. My father turned on the headlights and stretched, resting his arm along the back of the seat. "Are you ready to get back home?" he asked. I nodded, sleepy, content, talked out. His big hand rested briefly on the back of my head, playfully tugging at my braided ponytail until the pickup was in reverse. We were silent on the short ride back. The warm glow of the kitchen light gleamed softly, bidding us welcome.

When I crawled back into bed that night, little did I realize how this Christmas would affect every Christmas for the rest of my life. The memory would be relived over and over countless times, an unwritten poem with no words befitting description. I seldom take a sip of coffee without thinking of the very first time I tasted it, and at the arrival of each December, I start searching for the dancing lights, still amazed at their mystic beauty but curious as to why they have never matched the brilliance of their display that night so many years ago when I sat with my father on a quiet hill in the country, and we wrote our names in the sky by the lights that danced from earth to heaven.

Reel Event

By B.J. Taylor

"Do we have to watch that one again?" I pleaded as the rest of the room erupted in laughter. There I was at nine years old, dancing in front of the camera, with gangly arms and legs, straight bangs, and a wide grin showing an embarrassing gap in the front of my mouth.

"Look at you B.J.! Your two front teeth are missing!"

"Yeah, yeah, yeah," I said to the room filled with relatives. "You say that every time."

Watching those old home films was like watching a Wizard of Oz movie before they added color. And there wasn't any sound, either. Dad used to have the camera in his hand at every Christmas, birthday, picnic and family event. When it was turned on, everyone seemed to be possessed. They jerked around like marionettes on strings, pulling their lips wide with their fingers and grinning up close to the camera, or putting two fingers in the shape of a V behind their sister's or brother's head just to make Mom yell at them to stop. Nothing missed the eye of the camera. Not even Uncle Frank walking out of the bathroom trailing toilet paper stuck to the bottom of his shoe.

Later, when color film came out, we'd howl with laughter as we watched Dad in his plaid polyester pants and thick, black-rimmed glasses. Mom was no slouch in the fashion department, either. Dad captured her perfect 1960's image in a teased, upswept hairdo with her version of plaid played out in shorts with matching blouses.

It took Dad a while to get everything set up the night of our big movie showing event. He lugged out the heavy projector and placed it on a card table, then used books under the feet to prop it up just right. We walked around the room pulling the shades down and closing the drapes. Dad tested the square beam of light as it hit the living room wall where just moments before a picture of the Grand Canyon used to be. We gazed in amazement as he moved the card table forward then back, getting the image to just the right size and the focus as clear as he could make it.

These nights were as special as the movies we came to see. The ladies brought cold cuts, potato salad, pickles, olives, cut up veggies and brownies for dessert. While Dad reloaded the projector between flicks, you could sneak into the kitchen to reload your plate. "Come on!" someone would shout from the living room. "It's starting!" The cold cut grazers would dash to the doorway as the characters flickered to life.

We shared laughter and tears as we watched reels and reels of film showing old pets, old houses, and old friends. The threads of our life were captured in each metal can with a white label on top. There was Connie's First Birthday, Joey's Baptism, and The Family Vacation to Disneyland. But the one we all clamored to see was the one labeled "Station Demolition." It was the razing of Dad's old building on his corner lot to make way for a new building. He stood across the street and filmed the implosion.

The first time we saw the building crumble down as it played out on the wall, we let loose with *ooohhs* and *aaahhs*. But then someone had the bright idea to play it backwards. Throwing the projector into reverse, we all watched as the building rose from the pile of rubble to become whole again. Oh, it was great and we all hollered, cheered and clapped. "Play it again, Daddy!" And he did, first forward with *ooohhs* and *aaahhs* and then in reverse with cheers and clapping. Dad showed incredible patience, but finally ran out after the fifth or sixth time and we would watch the building collapse and stay that way.

It was the saddest part of movie night to hear the final reel play out with its flap, flap, flap as it spun until the projector was turned off. "That's all folks," Dad would say as he shut it down for the night.

Each round metal can held yards of memories and were treasured as family mementos usually are. Kept in a cardboard box tucked in a corner of the basement next to the projector, we always knew right where they were for the next time movie night rolled around.

Then one day the pipes burst and water flooded the basement. "Oh, Dad, all our movies are ruined. We'll never see the station demolition again!" I cried.

"Don't you worry, sweetheart. We can replay that movie forward and backward right up here," he said, tapping the side of his head. "Right up here."

It's been many years since that day we lost all our old film and many more since Dad died, too. Even though we may lose something we treasure and love, even when we cannot touch it or feel it in our hands it is still there—in our minds and in our hearts. Now that's a REAL event.

"Nothing in the world can take the place of persistence. Talent will not; nothing is more common than unsuccessful men with talent. Genius will not; unrewarded genius is almost a proverb. Education will not; the world is full of educated failures. Persistence and determination alone are omnipotent."

– Calvin Coolidge

The Fall Line

By Tom Pawlak

After a long Friday of business meetings in Chicago, the conversation turned to personal plans for the weekend. I cringed somewhat while mentioning that "I'm flying to Buffalo to go skiing with my dad."

As I waited for the usual reaction, someone said, "How nice...and your dad still skis, that's terrific.... How old is he?"

"He passed away years ago," I responded, "but, each year I fly home on his birthday and ski his favorite ski trail with him. The family scattered his ashes there. Skiing along that trail has become a yearly tradition."

The room fell silent as the other 50-ish business men and women thought about what I just said. They weren't thinking about Buffalo. They were all lost in thoughts of their own fathers.

My father's name is Ed. He grew up one of seven kids in a Polish immigrant family. Raised in a poor working-class section of Buffalo, he had an odd dream of working for the U.S. Forest Service. He loved the outdoors, sailing the lake, exploring the coastline, and above all else, the snowy hills South of Buffalo. Growing up he read about the explorers of his generation. Roald Amundsen, the first man to reach the North Pole, was one of his favorites. At age 13 he would travel the 30 or so miles to those snow filled hills, strap on wooden skis, and teach himself to ski.

He had a vision few shared at the time. Outdoor adventure meant speeding down snow covered slopes. Today he would have been labeled an X-treme Sportsman. He did something that Polish boys from Buffalo didn't do. Back then skiing was the sport of elite young blue-bloods from Dartmouth and Colgate. He startled many of those people when he came in second at the NY State Ski Competition. He was very much his own man.

One sunny summer day he met my mom, who was 16, and working at a shop on the Lake Erie beach. He asked her for cigarettes and a canoe ride on the lake. His greatest adventure had just started.

I wish I could say that my father's life was filled only with happiness or that all his dreams came true. The Second World War came. My father enlisted in the 10th Mountain Division and was assigned to Camp Hale in Colorado as a ski instructor and mountaineer. He loved every second of his time in the Rockies. The Division was shipped to Italy and received the highest casualty rate of any U.S. Division as it broke through the Poe River Valley. Bob Dole was in his Company. Bob and my father were seriously wounded.

Wounded, however, is an understatement. My father was hit by a grenade while trying to bring ammunition to his platoon. It was a devastating Purple Heart injury. A year later he lay in Valley Forge Hospital still riddled with shrapnel; even the bandages made him sick, giving him horrible rashes. When they finally sent him home to my mother, he was a different man.

At that time there wasn't any term like "post traumatic shock syndrome." Back then you just came home. "God bless you. We love you for what you did…now just get on with your life." Ed did his best to get on with his life as before, but the world had changed. He enrolled in college to study forestry; rashes prevented him from doing his old job; my brother arrived and he needed to make a living. He was offered a job as a draftsman. Reluctantly, he took the job. The outdoors became a skylight and the pickax became a drafting pencil. *Ed had the courage to alter his dream for my mother, my brother, and eventually me.*

So years later when I started to walk, my dad brought me to those same mountains where he had found his dreams of outdoor adventure. He put skis on my feet, pointed me down the hill, and said, "Go on down son. You'll like this."

I went from being scared to loving the excitement of speed and control. My dad showed me how to make skiing a waltz along the mountains fall line. He loved the precision of the sport; he was a perfectionist when it came to skiing technique. We skied together as a family every weekend of the long Buffalo winters.

I never followed my dad's footsteps; I'm not a draftsman, or a forest ranger, but I love the outdoors and skiing. Once a year I return to where my father stood at the top of the mountain, surrounded by blue sky, crisp air and packed powder snow. I see his eyes as clear now as I saw them as a child. I hear his voice, feel his enthusiasm, and follow him one more time…down the fall line of the mountain. We ski together, turning, banking into perfectly controlled turns. As my speed increases, my style improves. I can feel Ed right there watching, guiding, helping, and loving his son. The adventure continues to this day.

I will ski that run with him every year for the rest of my life. My father gave me more than he will ever know. He gave me the freedom of finding the fall line of life and traversing it with courage.

Grace

By Leanne Krause

"Your father helped me save my life. He was a great, great man," a stocky, middle-aged woman said, shaking my hand for nearly half a minute. My brothers and I stood in the receiving line at the funeral home while our father lay in his Newport Poplar box with a faint smile wearing a pin striped suit, his horn-rimmed glasses still perched on his nose.

My brother Jon and I had each touched his hand, curious to see what an actual dead person felt like. It was cold and hard. When we stared long enough, he appeared to be breathing. The funeral director told us that our minds were accustomed to seeing him alive, and still trying to fool us into believing that he was. He wore his gold wedding band, his Columbia University ruby ring, and one other piece of jewelry he always kept on his lapel—his pewter camel pin, for good luck. "If a camel can go for days without a drink," he used to say, "then so can I."

My father was an anesthesiologist who had become an addiction recovery physician. Our family life had been re-shuffled in my teen years, when he decided that a glass of wine at dinner might not be a bad idea. A year later he was a stranger to us, with his martini-percodan cocktails and his fender benders. We became accustomed to his numerous attempts to give up and stay sober on his own, each time sliding back further until he wound up tied to a table at a recovery center in Maryland. His Chief of Staff position was gone, and our family was reduced to depression and anger through the most difficult Christmas we'd ever had.

While I was graduating from college, my father was also graduating from a treatment center in New Jersey, where he'd moved after his initial stay in Maryland. Humbled by his experience, he clung to his Book of Devotions on trips home. He had bonded with the people at the hospital and, combining his interest in psychology with his propensity to tell people what to do, got a job as a counselor there. In time, he became a licensed Doctor of Alcoholism and, eventually, Medical Director of a treatment center in Pennsylvania.

During our phone conversations my father always checked to see if I'd found a good Adult Children of Alcoholics meeting, which I did now and then. Once he invited me to attend the Family Program at his workplace, to see what I could further discover about myself. During that week, he let me secretly listen to an intake conversation with a new patient who was outraged at having been sent there. My father responded with the same calm voice I remembered as a child; the one that could cut through a mire of illusion and accept no nonsense; the one that would pause to take a deep breath and tell someone on the operating table to start counting backwards from one hundred; the one that cheerfully remembered every nurse's name, and the one that explained logically why there could not be a 500-pound gorilla hiding in my bedroom closet at night. The best part of that week was watching him deliver his morning lecture to the entire treatment center. He spoke openly about his own experience, communicating a sense of hope and possibility. He was inspiring, animated, and totally happy. I could not remember a time when my father looked so complete. When the lecture was over I glanced around at the people in the audience and saw that they were all smiling and uplifted, as they began to discuss with each other the shifts necessary to continue with their lives.

My father became a better version of himself through his experience, although it was a rockier path than he might have chosen in retrospect. During apparent misfortune I've learned to look for the blessing that often hides behind it. When I face an obstacle I feel encouraged to take a different perspective. After my father's death I could not help but imagine that he had fulfilled his mission on earth. In the face of adversity, he turned a corner in his professional life and recognized his talent in communicating with people. He was a leader in the fledgling field of addiction recovery in the late 1970's; historically a subject more often discouraged or kept private.

My brothers and I stayed next to the casket with our father's wife for six hours that day, shaking the hands of hundreds who came to pay their respects. A constant stream of people all said the same essential thing to us: "Your father helped me save myself."

The Art of Patience

By Linda E. Allen

Yes, I'm a self-confessed Daddy's girl. Maybe it's because my dad and I shared the same birthday—the 23rd of July on his 23rd birthday, and I was his first child. And, maybe I was indeed an especially spoiled child. Admittedly, we had a special bond for the years we shared.

Even though he is physically gone, the lessons he taught continue beyond his earthly life. Of course, there were the lessons of honor, responsibility, doing your best, and being true to yourself that many dads teach. Words like "If everyone else is doing it, that's probably a good reason why you shouldn't do it" echo in my memory as I admonish my own children with the same words. They make much more sense now as an adult than when I was a teenager with an attitude and an agenda.

My dad could discipline with a look, referred to lovingly by his grandsons as the "Crawford look," after his middle name. Somewhat like an evil eye, it was a look that spoke volumes without saying a word and would instantly quiet my sassy mouth and tone, letting me know I had trespassed beyond his line of tolerance. If I dared continue my misbehavior beyond the "look," I knew I would be dealing with appropriate and deserved consequences. No, my dad was not profane, vulgar, or obscene in his language nor abusive in his behavior, but firm and strict with a follow-through that would not budge no matter how many tears or how much cajoling and manipulating I tried. These were perhaps some of the first lessons of patience, persistence, and determination he taught me. Our family called it stubbornness or bull-headedness, but the lessons were deep and lasting.

One of the favorite memories of his grandsons was the time they were working with him to repair a stubborn boat motor with little success. Instead of throwing tools, cursing, or swearing, he methodically and patiently worked, testing and retesting each piece and part until he had solved the problem. He told them there was no need to get angry or upset over a boat motor because, after all, he was smarter than the motor, and he just had to prove it. What an amazing lesson in patience, persistence, and determination in action!

My dad was like all human dads with his share of problems, challenges and faults that taught me as much as his positive characteristics. But, he always seemed superhuman to me, especially in later years, overcoming all kinds of physical problems and challenges after a stroke with all its complications and frustrations changed his lifestyle. For 14 years, this once vital, strong and independent man depended on others to do for him what most of us take for granted. Even though his mobility and speech were severely limited, quite possibly this part of his life became his greatest teaching example.

A special gift from God at this time in his life was his art—a talent he developed from simple sketches to finely detailed animal portraits. Although he had sketched house plans on napkins and backs of envelopes that turned out just as he designed them, he had no formal art training or experience even as a hobby. His career had been in airplane mechanics and troubleshooting.

It all began when my mother gave him a pencil and some paper and encouraged him to draw as a way to occupy his time and to help regain the skills the stroke had stolen from him. His first attempt was like that of a child, a simple outline, but easily recognizable as a fish. Over a period of years, he worked with determined dedication at his art, his left hand steadily and slowly stroking the page with graceful lines—always done in a #2 lead pencil. He almost always drew animals, especially dogs, and his drawings became highly detailed animals with each hair or strand of fur individually and lovingly birthed from his imagination and memory. With patience and practice, his talent blossomed, and his animals took on personalities that invited others in his nursing center to stop by his table to watch the man whose talent had been released by his stroke. The searching and often sad eyes of his subjects seemed to tell stories from the pages of his sketchbook, expressing the thoughts and emotions he could no longer speak.

Patience, persistence, and determination, the characteristics that had guided his pre-stroke life, were poignantly obvious as he worked day after day creating his animals. "A job well done is a job done well" now became a lesson to others as they watched a man overcoming his limitations with grace and dignity, gradually proving that practice (plus patience, persistence, and determination) does makes perfect. From his simple sketches evolved artwork that gave meaning to his life and contributed beauty to his world. He enjoyed sharing his art with others and the happiness it gave them.

In the twilight hours of his life, when he and I both knew that death was waiting in the shadows to release him from his suffering, we were granted the gift of a final conversation. Actually, I did all the talking since his speech was gone and his energy drained. He could only listen as I talked about our special times together and shared the memories that meant so much to me. I had a special time to say all those things we each know we should say but many times put off until later. This time was the later I had neglected and avoided. I told my dad how much I loved him, how blessed I am to be his daughter and how much he had taught me throughout his life.

His response to me was a soft, slow smile while he drew a circle in the air. To me it was a sign that his life had come full circle and that he was leaving this world at peace, the same way he had entered. It was the passing of the torch, a rite of passage from one generation to the next, leaving me the legacy of his lessons of patience, perseverance, and determination to share with others and to practice in my own life. Thank you, Daddy.

"Adversity has the effect of eliciting talents which,
in prosperous circumstances,
would have lain dormant."
- Horace

Where There's a Will, There's a Way

By Renie (Szilak) Burghardt

Before World War II put an end to it all, my grandparents, who raised me, and I had been a prosperous family in our country; Hungary. Apa, my grandfather, who was the only father I knew, was a judge in the village where we lived, while Grandmother ran the General Store. They also owned a farm where I often watched Apa till the soil with the help of his two oxen. He never shrank from hard work, and he took great pride in providing well for his family. Then—*poof*—the war came and everything was gone, just like that!

When the war ended, life did not improve for the people of Hungary. Soviet occupation and the new communist government brought with it new atrocities. Because Apa spoke out against these atrocities, he was soon in danger of being imprisoned. We fled to freedom in the late fall of 1947.

A refugee camp in neighboring Austria then became our new home. Called a Displaced Persons Camp, D.P Camp Spittal an der Drau (on the Drau) housed hundreds of destitute refugees. Although dismal and cramped, we were grateful to God that the camp provided a roof over our heads, and we were clothed with donated goods, and fed cabbage and potato soup daily. So what did it matter that we didn't have a penny to our name?

However, it mattered a great deal to Apa. He hated living off the charity of others; hated not being able to buy me the book I had glanced at longingly when we passed a bookstore in town. But what could he do about it? He had no other option.

Just beyond our dismal camp home was another world—a beautiful, natural world of mountains, clear, cold streams, rolling flower-carpeted hills, and small farms dotted with grazing animals. It was this other world that ignited my imagination with its beauty and gave my heart hope. So I often slipped away from the crowded world of the camp, and roamed the hills and valleys, explored and grew to love nature, and filled my stomach with wild blueberries or other of nature's offerings. On one of my rambles, I discovered the beautiful river Drau, just a half-mile walk from the camp, where I would sit mesmerized, gazing at the surrounding mountains, and dreaming my childish dreams of better days. It became my favorite retreat, and one day I told Apa about it.

"A river?" he asked with great interest. "How far is this river from the camp?"

"I'm not sure, but it takes me a half-an-hour to walk to it," I replied.

"Good. Tomorrow I'll go to the river with you."

"Oh, you will love it, Apa," I said enthusiastically. "It's the Drau River, and it is so beautiful!"

"I have always loved rivers. Rivers benefit animals and people," he replied thoughtfully.

The following morning, Apa and I set out on our walk to the river Drau. Once we reached it, I splashed around in the shallow, clear, rushing water, while he walked up and down the bank. After a while, I noticed that he was cutting some branches from the river willows growing all along the bank. By the time we headed back to the camp, he had a large armful of them.

"What are you going to do with them?" I asked him, on our way back to the camp.

"I will make some baskets," Apa replied. Suddenly, I remembered that in the past, Apa's hobby had been weaving. He had made a beautiful settee for Grandma, and an adorable table and chair for me when I was five. But in the course of the war, all that had been forgotten.

"And what will you do with the baskets?" My curiosity was aroused.

"I will try and sell them to the Austrians."

Soon, Apa found some old boards and bricks, and set up a worktable in front of the barrack. Then after peeling the willow branches, he began weaving his first basket. A large crowd gathered around to watch him. Some boys volunteered to get more willow branches for him.

"Thank you," Apa told them. "And when I sell my baskets, I will pay you for your help."

Within a short time, there were six beautifully woven baskets ready for market. Apa hung them on a long stick, flung them over his shoulder, and (to my grandmother's dismay) looking like a hobo peddler, off he went to town. He returned a few hours later with the hobo stick minus the baskets. He had sold all of them! Then he reached into his pocket and pulled something out, handing it to me. It was the new book I had been longing for!

"Oh, thank you, Apa," I shrieked, giving him a hug. "I can't believe you were able to buy it."

"You are very welcome. And never forget—where there is a will, there is always a way," he said. Then he went off to pay the boys who had helped him gather the willow branches.

Apa continued with his new venture all summer, and even gave free lessons in basket weaving to anyone interested. After he sold the next batch of baskets, he bought himself a fishing pole, too, and a large frying pan, and building a fire outside the barrack, cooked a batch of the large fish he caught in the beautiful Drau River, and shared it with our neighbors. (Later, he shared the fishing pole and frying pan as well!) It was most unusual to have the aroma of that frying fish wafting through the camp, where barracks were lined up like soldiers, and helpless people lived their lives in them, hoping and praying for something better.

My dear Apa's example was an inspiration to many at that camp. His motto became my motto in life, and it has always served me well!

Coming Up Roses

By Peri Shawn

I remember my favorite day with my dad as if it were yesterday. We talked all day on the topic of souls passing into the next world. I loved to listen to him when he got going about spiritual things.

He talked about the difference between our body's and our soul's sense of time. He spoke of the recent passing of his best friend. Dad had expected that at the exact moment of his friend's passing, he would have some internal knowing of his death. He didn't. It wasn't until days later that Dad felt the leaving of his friend's soul. Dad was at the house at the time. It felt like a storm was coming when a rush of humid air circled around the house. As it left, he heard his friend's voice say, "I made it, Doug."

As usual, our time together that day ended much later than we had planned. We hugged and said our good-byes.

Dad always encouraged me to be independent. At the age of thirteen, I traveled on my own for a week in the States.

After my trip, he picked me up at the bus station. In the car on the way back home, he asked question after question, going over *every* detail of my trip.

When we got back to the house, he encouraged me to go to my room to unpack. And there on my dresser was a dozen miniature peach colored roses with a note that read, "Welcome home, Doll." Doll was his nickname for me. I was touched.

The roses became *our* tradition after each of my trips—his special homecoming for me, always prefaced with him picking me up and asking me question after question about my trip.

When I was a university student, I worked in Banff for a summer. That summer was the hardest summer for me. Shortly after I had left, my boyfriend of three years had found another "doll" to play with.

My dreams were shattered. My boyfriend and I had planned to get married when I finished university. My future, in my eyes, was with him. And now I didn't see a future.

Dad knew that I was heart broken. He wrote me many letters that summer. Oh, how I wanted to go home. And to my surprise, he encouraged me to stay in Banff.

Dad said that there would always be tests and difficulties in my life. That tests and difficulties wouldn't go away. It was how I perceived my tests and difficulties that would make the difference to my life. And this was my opportunity to truly learn this lesson. Tests and difficulties were the fuel for the development of friendships and growth. He said if I focused on the friendships and growth that I would start to see things differently. Coming home was not the solution. It would be my focus that was the solution, not my location.

I stayed. And I *did* begin to see things differently.

When I finally came home at the end of that summer, as usual, Dad picked me up. On the car ride back, as usual, he asked his question after question. We pulled into the driveway and he stopped before getting out of the car. This was not usual. He turned to me and gave me a knowing look and with a twinkle in his eye, he said, "You made it, Doll."

At that moment I did feel proud of myself and my choices, proud of my growth, proud of my new friendships. And most of all, proud that I had internalized the important lesson that the quality of my life was not based on where I was physically but rather my focus—that tests and difficulties are a gift for the development of friendships and growth.

When we entered the house Dad asked, "Don't you have some bags to unpack?" I had forgotten about our tradition. Now it was *me* who had the twinkle in the eye. I rushed to my room in search of my miniature peach colored roses. And, the twinkle in my eye turned to a tear. There were no miniature peach colored roses.

Well, there *was* the note that read, "Welcome Home Doll." And behind it, instead of my dozen miniature peach colored roses, there were a dozen Oceania roses. Same color, but much larger and far more fragrant. They were gorgeous.

The tear? This time I finally got the real meaning. "Home," in Dad's note, now was not the external place but an internal place. And the roses represented a stepping-stone to my internal home—a step further on my personal journey of growth. The roses were an external reward for my internal growth.

At 11:00 p.m. on that favorite day with Dad, I got the news that I was the last person on Earth to see him.

I was numb.

To console myself I took out my box of pictures and there on top was a picture of me at my university graduation with roses in my arms…you guessed it, Oceania roses from Dad. In my head came the familiar advice that went with tests and difficulties - focus on friendships and growth. Friendships and growth.

The night after Dad's passing, as I lay in my bed, I felt a change in the air. It was a pressure change—humid and still. It *certainly* had my attention. Then I clearly heard Dad's voice say, "I made it, Doll. I made it."

Of course, he'd made it. His life was about taking continual steps to his internal home. His life was focused on rich friendships and growth. So yes, his whole life was a series of steps to his internal home. You made it, Dad.

The next day I ordered the flowers for the top of Dad's casket. The florist, not sure that she understood me correctly, asked me to repeat my order. "Yes," I said, "you did hear me correctly. I did say a dozen Oceania roses."

Unspoken Lessons

By Patricia Asaad

Henry Girner could have portrayed himself as a hero in the face of hardships. A martyr who overcame every challenge sent his way. As an adoring daughter, I would have hung on every word. Such stories might have shamed me into being a better person—temporarily. But he never did any of those things. He refused to talk about himself and that silence screamed louder than any speech. His example became the beacon I needed during my own storms, when I needed strength to overcome obstacles.

Most of the fragments I knew about his life came from my mother. He always answered my questions, and talked to me at length about other topics, but he didn't enjoy talking about himself. At the time, I interpreted it as disinterest, but now I'd say it was hurt.

My grandfather had died when my dad was eight years old. It was at the height of the Great Depression and his mother could not support the family nor could she find any family members to help. Through a series of events, my dad ended up spending most of his childhood in an orphanage. After high school, he went into the Air Force, became a bomber pilot in World War II, and made it all the way to major by the end of the war. He commanded his squadron even though he was the youngest man in it.

After the war, he earned an engineering degree and went to work for an oil company, only to learn that younger men, who hadn't spent all those years in the war, got the promotions. I never heard him rant about the unfairness of it all; he just came up with a plan. By this time, he had married and had three little girls to support so he went into business for himself.

He bought an almost bankrupt car dealership, and turned it into the largest and most successful dealership in town.

His success in business was not without a price; he worked seven days a week and many nights he didn't return until long after I'd gone to bed. I remember saying, "I never want to work that hard," and his reply was always, "Anything in life worth doing won't be easy," and he graciously ignored a prime opportunity to lecture me on the value of hard work.

Shortly after buying the dealership, a man who had been in his squadron during the war recognized my dad from a newspaper article and came to visit us. I saw the man hold my mother's hand and tell her my dad was a great man. He said my dad was brave and honorable and through his courage and sound judgment, had saved the lives of his men. I felt my heart swell with pride and I asked to hear the stories of his heroic adventures, but again, he would not talk about it. He only said that war was not pretty, he didn't want to glorify it and he'd only done what he had to do.

Many times, I've looked at his life and thought nothing ever came easy to him. He could have harbored bitterness and complained, but he didn't. I never saw my dad quit anything no matter how difficult. Growing up, I didn't stop and think about these things, but somehow they burrowed into my consciousness to be available for later use.

Eventually I finished college, got a job and moved away from home, but something was wrong. Every day I dragged home. Feeling weak, achy and feverish, I'd crawl up the stairs to my apartment. After weeks of a daily fever and host of other symptoms, I took a leave of absence from my job and went home to stay with my parents. They went with me to numerous doctor appointments. After a battery of tests, the doctors diagnosed me with systemic lupus.

At 22-years-of-age, looking forward to a life of fever, fatigue, and pain overwhelmed me. And that was only if the disease didn't attack a major organ and kill me first. For several days, depression pressed in on me. I thought my life would never be good again. But before long, the messages from my upbringing came into focus. I knew what I had to do, without words; my dad had taught me the lessons years ago.

No matter how bad I felt, I still needed to persevere. Self-pity was not an option, neither was complaining. The only way not to become self-absorbed was to focus on others and meet their needs. His lessons worked.

I still run a fever every day. Some days I don't have the strength to sit up, and it feels like a knife is twisting in my joints. But I'm amazed at how good my life is. I'm happily married, I have two loving teenage sons, and I've found a fulfilling career with the flexibility I need to work around my health issues. I look at my life and I'm happy.

Having a chronic illness could have ruined my chances for joy, but seeing my dad's example of perseverance prepared me for difficulties in ways I couldn't have learned from mere words. If he'd lectured me and lifted himself up as some sort of unreachable ideal, I only would have become more aware of my shortcomings and lost confidence. I would have grown to resent him and been unprepared for my life.

Even death did not come easily for my father. For a year and a half, he battled colon cancer, enduring surgery after surgery and numerous rounds of chemotherapy and radiation. Eventually, he became too weak to get out of bed, but he still fought.

Characteristic of his mind-set, the last thing I heard him say was that he was grateful for his good life. Then he lapsed into a coma. The hospice workers told us he didn't have long, but he held on for another week. It was as if he couldn't let go. He couldn't speak, but I thought I knew what was bothering him. He was worried about my mom. When I whispered to him that I was living at the house so I could be there for Mom, he let go. He'd held on until he knew she would have someone there.

Like everything else he had done, he refused to quit. When I think about his life, his determination shines through in every memory. I picture him pushing through difficult times and never complaining nor boasting about it. So many times the most helpful lessons are the unspoken ones.

I'm sure my dad would have loved to make my disease go away, but he did something so much better. His example taught me to grow through trials. I dream of perfect health, but I wonder if I'm happier now than I would have been without lupus. In order to cope, I've had to grow so much in my character that it has improved my outlook on everything.

Still when my children are hurting, I worry about saying the right thing. I want to fix it. Then I remember my dad. They don't need for all their problems to go away or hours of advice. They are absorbing messages I would never think to communicate because striving to live by convictions is the most powerful lesson a parent can give.

"Men are only great as they are kind."

– Elbert Hubbard

Mess Sergeant Muzzy, U.S.M.C.

By Thomas Edward

When I was a boy, my dad would take me hunting above the Ballville Dam through the standing corn for ring-neck pheasants and cottontail rabbits. My Ryder Lever Action BB gun inadvertently pointed toward my dad, I whined "Can't I have a shotgun like yours?" Pushing my weapon's barrel away and obviously irritated, he replied, "Hell's Bells! I gotta teach you the difference between your gun and your weapon first." Next Christmas brought joy with a 20 gauge Winchester shotgun. My manhood was initiated by my hunting instructor, baseball coach, scout master, football coach, fishing buddy, and later, house painter, carpenter, mason, electrician, plumber, and jack-of-all-trades—Sergeant Muzzy, U.S.M.C.

My dad was orphaned and raised by older brothers and sisters during the Depression. After high school football practice, maybe he would find a cold boiled potato. It probably perked his interest in cooking later. His nickname "Muzzy" bestowed after his football coach could not pronounce the Polish name of his fearless 140 pound dynamo, who single-handedly stopped a future All-American one entire game. Dad joined the U.S.M.C., did his boot camp at Quantico just before WWII, and was one of the first 100 marines sent to establish Parris Island as a boot camp. Having played semi-pro baseball, the Corps wanted him on their team as shortstop. He chose instead to ship out overseas with his outfit. He married my mom, his high school sweetheart, while on furlough. I was born in the baby boom while he was island hopping in the Pacific.

The War campaigns took longer than anticipated as the Japanese were determined to fight until the last man. After weeks of Marine spearhead invasions, food was a monotonous and repetitious as the war. Field mess cooks did what they could to feed hungry Marines out of combat seeking a bit of respite. Complaints were frequent as the canned spam, powdered eggs and milk, rations, dried foods, and the usual meal fare became unpalatable.

Mess Corporal Muzzy picked up the gauntlet when complaints became up front and personal. He got an idea watching all the activity of the Navy ships in the harbor. The Navy had refrigeration, and their food was the best quality in the service. He asked the combat Marines in his mess to bring back all the souvenirs they could find and promised them a new menu. He enlisted a Seabee friend with an LST (Landing Ship, Tank) and displayed the collected souvenirs in the bottom of the water craft including Japanese flags, swords, officer pistols, and even a "Namu" machine gun. They leisurely embarked and made the rounds through the harbor fleet to see if there was any interest in their accumulated booty. On the first pass, naval officers were hailing, bartering, even begging for these souvenirs not in reach from their ships. "No money!" Corporal Muzzy clearly stated, "I need fresh and frozen food for my mess."

The Navy was most generous and accommodating and filled his LST almost to the gunnels with frozen turkeys and steaks, strawberries, vegetables, desserts, even ice cream, fresh frozen breads and butters and everything combat-worn Marines had not seen for months. A three-day feast ensued at Muzzy's mess as the word quickly spread. Marines walked, drove, and hitched rides in from miles away for a fresh hot meal from good old Ski's mess. It wasn't long after that Corporal Muzzy made Sergeant. Marines also travel on their stomachs and his officers rewarded the enterprising corporal with a promotion when his mess was recognized as the best in the field. Hurrah for Sergeant Muzzy! He only worried that, since the Navy made him sign for the entire lot of food, one day the government would knock on his door and demand payment for the groceries the Navy lent to the Marines.

The Invasion of Japan and the last big battle Okinawa featured 4,000 Kamikaze "human bombs," and tore up the fleet with the highest battle causalities of the entire war. And it appeared it was going to be a very long war. Truman saw the coast in terms of American lives and let the Japanese decide after nuking two of their cities. Sarge watched the surrender signing on the U.S.S. *Missouri*. He smiled as he related how the Japanese surrender party had to walk between two rows of hand-picked men from all branches of the armed services. They were chosen for their height and size. The smaller Japanese were taken aback by the goliaths they had been fighting. Never again would they "awake a sleeping giant," in the words of Admiral Yamamoto.

Sarge mustered out of the Marine Corps at Cherry Point, NC after finishing out his second tour of duty (6 years total). He began the transition back to civilian life trying many jobs, and we floated about a good deal. My mother's parents came to our rescue. Two families under one roof can lead to conflicts, and we had ours, but we settled in, planted a garden, grew crops, and bartered for eggs and milk. Mom and "Gramma" home-canned fruits and vegetables. Dad painted houses and did a variety of construction-related work. I mowed lawns, set pins at a bowling alley, and delivered newspapers. Dad and I caught snapping turtles and sold the meat for soup, and grew fishing worms to be sold in late summer when none were available. We did anything to put a few dollars in the till. The money was used for family needs and even a vacation trip to see his Marine buddy, "Pappy," and his family in Buffalo, NY. I wonder now whether they ever had time to reminisce about their experiences with screaming kids, barbeque fires, bean hole beans, and beer with cries of "Fire in the hold!" alerting the neighborhood of fireworks and/or beans ready to go off simultaneously.

He persevered in his allegiance (Semper Fidelis—*Always Faithful*) joining the Marine Corps League and becoming a member of the honor guard team for funerals, ball games, 4th of July, Veteran's Day, etc. The Marine Corps Reserve was another matter. Many of his buddies joined for the extra money and had to face the Korean War. Dad was tempted but wisely avoided the Reserves. Instead he researched sourdough pancakes, the original recipe, and the intricacies of keeping the starter and creating a truly amazing original "flap-jack." He started the monthly Marine Pancake Breakfast Mess for old buddies and new Marines alike with revelry, a flag raising with a carbide canon salute.

After I completed college and at the height of the Viet Nam conflict, I decided to carry on the proud tradition in the family and enlist in the Marine Corps. Dad's reaction was startling. "Like hell you will. I fought 6 years in WWII so you would not have to go." It was a compelling argument. I was his only son and the only one to carry on his family name.

Over the years, we lost our close connection. Time and distance cast a shadow between us and drew us farther apart and on different paths. Dad's spark of life slowly diminished and it was cancer that did at long last, what war, deprivation, and life's hard knocks could not do. After many medical battles, he answered his final bugle call.

We had always shared a mutual love of sports, especially football. Shortly after his death, I was watching a New England Patriots football game on their way to a Super Bowl Championship. Things looked bleak. So I decided to pray to my dad, who was now closer to Divine intercession. Crazy as it may seem, every time I asked for help, it came through— time and time again. I know he was helping. I could almost hear him saying, "Hell's Bells and jingles, my boy we can't lose. Who's your Daddy? The Marine Corps was mine and do you remember their hymn? I would sing it to you as I rocked you to sleep. It is like a prayer that inspires inward confidence and a clear rallying point to duty and the task at hand. And as surely as you have my blood flowing in your veins, you are my protégé, my legacy, and my liege."

Then on the first anniversary of his death, I had a Mass said for him in his home parish in the Midwest. My wife and I went to mass at our parish 1,000 miles away in New England. And who has our mass in the absence of our vacationing new pastor—a Marine chaplain friend of our pastor. What a coincidence! Tears came to my eyes as waves of nostalgia overcame me and these episodes from his life were clearly relived again and again in my mind. The sad thing is I so wanted to tell him one thing that I never told him in life. I always wanted to say, but never had the courage or grit, "Dad, I love you, Sarge."

Peace for Pickles

By B.J. Taylor

She just appeared one day, looking sad-eyed and mournful, peering in through the glass patio door. Her silky fur was jet black and her eyes were as big as saucers. I gazed at her and spoke the thought that was running through my head, "My, you are in quite a pickle." This beautiful, regal cat was definitely pregnant. Her stomach was bulging and she appeared ready to give birth any day.

I was in a pickle, too. I had lost my father after a long illness, and my days and nights were no longer filled with phone calls and visits. My grief enveloped me, like a black cloud. Friends and family called on the phone, but I didn't want to talk to anyone and I didn't want to go out. All I wanted to do was sleep. I knew it was time to get over my grieving and begin to live life again, but how could I do that when I couldn't even muster up my faith?

I sure didn't have the energy to take care of a cat. And a pregnant one at that. But I found myself pouring a small bowl of milk and opening the patio door. I set it outside. *She'll be gone by morning*, I thought. Pulling my bathrobe closer around me, I trudged back up the stairs and crawled into bed.

The next day she reappeared. *What is she doing back here? I can barely take care of myself right now, let alone a needy cat.* But I couldn't turn away. I found an old basket and arranged a soft blanket inside. I walked outside and she backed up about ten feet, watching me with wary eyes. I set down the basket and went back in the house.

Remembering my dad's caring ways was the only comfort I had right now. He loved animals, and had a soft spot in his heart for every stray.

When I was a little girl, our house was a revolving door for abandoned cats and dogs brought home by my dad after finding them in the restrooms of the gas station he owned. I could at least try to take care of her. Dad would like that. But only until I found out where she lived.

I had seen a black cat in our neighborhood, so I assumed she was someone's pet. On one of my furtive runs out to the mailbox in my worn out bathrobe and slippers, I saw my next-door neighbor.

"Hi, how are you?" he asked.

"Fine," I said as I ran my hand through my uncombed hair. "Can I ask you something? There's a black cat that's been coming around my backyard. Do you know where she lives?"

"That cat has been around for years. Everybody feeds her, but as far as I know, she doesn't have a home."

"Thanks," and I shuffled back inside with the mail clutched in my hand.

She was all alone, too. She must have had a hard life surviving on her own all those years.

"Okay, Dad, you must have guided her to my door. I'll take care of her," I spoke aloud.

I could almost hear him ask what I was going to call her.

"I'm going to name her Pickles."

I went upstairs to comb my hair. Looking in the bathroom mirror, I saw a wrinkled, creased face. *I wish somebody would take care of me*. Sadness etched the corners of my eyes and my shoulders sloped with the weight of grief I held there. The coolness of the water felt good as I ran a wet washcloth over my face. I changed out of my tired old bathrobe and put on jeans and a sweatshirt.

Over the next few days, Pickles came to drink the milk and eat the food I put out for her, but would then disappear. Each day I eagerly searched the basket for some sign of the new life Pickles was carrying. One morning, I saw a tiny black kitten curled up inside. Then I heard the screech of brakes.

"Oh, no!" I called out. There in the street was Pickles, running right in front of a car. She was carrying a solid gray kitten by the nape of its neck. Bounding across the yard, she deposited it in the basket and took off again. She made three more trips for a total of five kittens.

Cautiously, I made my way around the side of the house to get a closer look at the new babies. I longed to hold Pickles and snuggle her close, but her years of living in the wild made her wary of human contact. I peered into the basket and watched as she licked and cleaned each kitten. *They're finally here!*

Since Dad died, I had no one to take care of anymore. But now I couldn't wait to get up in the morning. The kittens needed me. I was showering, dressing, and even making my bed. I began to say hello to the neighbors when I went out for the mail, this time wearing real clothes instead of pajamas and a robe.

When I looked out through the patio door, I sure didn't feel alone when six pairs of hungry eyes stared back at me. I sat and played with the kittens for hours. It was such fun watching them roll around on top of each other and play hide n' seek under the edges of the blanket. I even started to laugh again, and was surprised when I heard that sweet, familiar sound. While Pickles watched from a distance, I stroked each furry little ball and soothingly crooned, "It's okay, Pickles. I won't hurt them. They're so cute with big eyes like yours and soft fur. Look at this one with the black and white mask on her face. She looks like a little bandit. And this solid black one looks just like you."

Pickles seemed to understand my contact with the kittens was necessary and it sure did my heart good. Sometimes, though, the sad tears would flow as I thought of how much I missed my dad. Then Pickles would look at me with those big eyes that seemed to say, *everything's going to be all right. You take care of me and I'll take care of you.*

When the kittens were old enough, I found homes for four of the five. The antics of every kitten endeared me to each one, but the solid gray one stood out among the rest. He was soft and cuddly, and I decided to keep him. When he stood up and stretched his paws against the door he looked just like a bear, so that's what I called him.

I guessed Pickles was around eight or nine years old and, according to the neighbors, she'd had more than a dozen litters. She was an excellent mother, but she looked exhausted after feeding, cleaning, and tending to her offspring. Now that the rest of the kittens were in new homes, I knew there was one more thing I needed to do. Pickles needed to be spayed, and Bear, too, when he was old enough.... Dad always told me how important that was. I decided to take Pickles to the vet so she could live the rest of her life in peace.

I thought it would be pretty easy, but she wouldn't go into a plastic cat carrier, no matter how much I tried to coax her. Unsure of what to do next, I prayed. *Dad, I need your help. I want Pickles to find peace. Please show me what to do.*

Later that day, I picked up the phone and called the vet's office. After explaining my dilemma, they said they had a metal cage I could borrow, which had a trap door used most often to catch wild animals that needed medical care.

I carried the cage to the backyard, and talked to Pickles, who sat in the corner watching me. "Look at this one, Pickles. It's much bigger and you can see through it. When you go inside, the door will shut behind you, but don't be afraid."

At the vet's suggestion, I placed a piece of chicken in the corner of the cage, with the metal door propped open. All Pickles had to do was approach the bait. What happened next seemed like a miracle. With a slow, steady gait, Pickles walked straight inside, almost as if a loving hand was guiding her. No backward glance, no hesitation, and no thrashing or trying to escape. Her weight pressed down on the spring and the door shut.

She sat inside, a calm surrounding her. Then it dawned on me. *Dad, was that your guiding hand?* I marveled at her acceptance and surrender. *Is that what it takes?* I wondered. *Acceptance?* Maybe that's what was lacking in my own life.

I brought her home from the vet the next day and let her out of the cage. She took a few steps, then turned and looked at me. Our eyes locked and I saw my own newfound serenity reflected in hers.

The gentle, guiding hand that showed Pickles the way to peace also showed me the way to acceptance. Dad always said that when you help others you forget about your own troubles. I found out he's right.

The Faith of My Father

By Sharon Tabor Warren

My entire life is filled with things my father taught me: patriotism, integrity, solid work ethic, sense of humor, and love of books are just a few. Recently, another tenet was brought to mind in a roundabout manner. Dad had an abiding faith that he lived, in today's jargon, twenty-four, seven. It was as much a part of him as his silver-white hair and twinkling blue eyes, his love of a good story and his khaki trousers. We always attended church and its various functions; we never considered playing hooky. I have to admit that many years of my adult life, I didn't go to church as I should have, but Dad never commented on my lapses. It wasn't that I'd forgotten his teaching; it was simply that I lived it each day in a subconscious way.

In our current church we have one member who likes to tell us what a good Christian he is. He related a story one morning of fixing a heater for a customer after his normal store hours because the temperatures were to drop overnight. I thought it was nice of him to do it but I wouldn't have bothered to stand in front of the congregation and tell the tale as an example of my Christianity. I probably wouldn't have bothered to ever tell the story; to me it would have been no more than holding a door open for someone—something as natural as breathing.

Dad taught me that you perform these little decencies—the catchphrase now is "random acts of kindness"—and you don't brag about them or expect praise. Your rewards will be in the good feeling you experience for having helped. Perhaps some day someone will help you out at a time of need, or you'll simply have more stars in your crown.

We moved to the California desert about halfway between Phoenix and Los Angeles right after World War II. It was a time when many people in the east migrated west, looking for the riches of the Golden State. Often the seekers were unprepared for the trip and resources were depleted by the time they reached us. Dad's name, address, and phone number were posted at the church for people to contact us in the event of emergency. The pastor's information was posted also, but our house and the church were both on numbered streets so we were easier to find than the parsonage.

Many a knock was heard and Dad would open the door to a veteran, sometimes alone, often with a wife and children. They were broke, needed food and gas. Dad gave them money, quite often from Mother's sugar bowl that held the household funds. The men muttered thanks with heads bowed, promised to send it back when they got work, and shuffled off into the night. Mother cried about her missing grocery money because she knew these lost souls never found the money to repay us.

Dad would say, "Don't worry about it, Irene. The Lord will provide." And He always did.

Dad never said a word to us about what he'd done. I remember asking once why these people needed help and he explained about car troubles, high food costs, sickness, and poor planning. He explained about the vets who'd fought so hard to protect us. Dad, too, was a veteran but he hadn't seen combat and I understood many years later he thought he owed a debt to those who had.

He never asked the church to reimburse him and he never used words like "Christian duty." He taught me to have a generous spirit and empathy for those who were less fortunate, not with his words, but by his example. He walked the walk and talked the talk.

Not a day passes that I don't miss him and his abiding wisdom.

The Lesson

By Jean Stewart

SCREECH...CRASH! The old black pickup truck in front of me stopped. I didn't. I slammed into its rear, crushing the fender and bending the driver's door of my car. Except that it wasn't my car. It was my father's. I shouldn't have been driving it, and now I had destroyed it.

The farmer climbed out of his truck slowly and deliberately and looked at the damage. I sat sobbing, my lip bleeding where I'd bitten it. He was quite concerned but we managed to exchange names and phone numbers before he pulled out onto the highway again. I cautiously followed, knowing I dared not go home. I'd be in big trouble.

It was my high school graduation day. I drove to school and crawled out through the passenger door. Surveying the mangled fender, contorted door, scrapes, and dents, tears flowed down my face, which was rapidly becoming more swollen by the minute—I didn't cry "pretty." I climbed up a ladder in the gym and began draping crepe paper for the dance that was to follow the ceremony. Word traveled fast and soon a teacher stood at my feet.

"You'll have to go home to get dressed sooner or later," she reasoned. "Sooner would be much better since you have to tell your parents."

It took her awhile, but I finally agreed and slowly drove home. The "Death March" sounded in my ears.

My mother took one look at my face when I walked in the door and screamed, "What on earth happened to you?"

I hung my head and tears spilled from my eyes again. "I crashed Daddy's car." She threw up her hands in dismay and rushed to the backyard where he was grilling burgers.

"Stop cooking, Ted. We're not going to eat. Jean has wrecked your car."

He looked at her and quietly said, "Is she hurt?"

"No, except for biting her lip."

"Well, then, what does that have to do with eating dinner?" He flipped a burger, piled it on a plate with the others, then walked across the yard and put his arm around me. "Let's go in and hear all about this—if you're sure you're all right."

I sniffled and nodded.

The phone was ringing when we got to the back door. The farmer wanted to make sure I was safe and had no other injuries. He refused to let Daddy pay for the scrapes on his truck.

I pressed ice to my lip while Mother brought cold washcloths for my swollen eyes. My father smiled at me and whispered, "Cars can be repaired…."

I graduated that evening with my family in attendance, joyful I had earned my diploma yet knowing my greatest lesson had come from my father. High school taught me what is important in books. Daddy taught me to value what is really important in life.

I smile in remembrance of that day and of him.

Treat Dad Like God This Father's Day

By Gregory J. Rummo

My dad passed away on December 27, 1996.

Two days prior—on Christmas morning—he was putting on his trousers, getting ready for church, when he slipped and fell, breaking his neck on the marble saddle separating the bedroom and bathroom.

I really lost both of my parents on that Christmas morning. Dad had been taking care of mom, who was in a slow spiral downwards from Alzheimer's disease. She was already past the point where he should have been her full-time caretaker. My wife and I were forced to put her in a nursing home on the day he died.

They would have celebrated their 55th wedding anniversary this past May.

My parents were happily married. But Dad had a "second wife" on the side that everyone knew about—music.

He was an accomplished pianist, a music teacher in the New York City public school system, a private vocal coach, and our church's organist and choir director.

I remember as a boy, hearing Dad struggle at the keyboard for months, trying to master Maurice Ravel's "Gaspard de la nuit." He told me that the third movement was so complicated even the composer himself had difficulty playing it.

Growing up in a home where the air was constantly filled with the strains of classical music undoubtedly fostered the desire to follow in my father's footsteps. So it's no surprise that I studied music and now play guitar, sing, and direct a choir in my church.

A dad is enormously important in the lives of his children. He is a role model to whom little eyes are constantly turning for guidance. Most boys look at their father and want to grow up and be "just like Daddy."

One of the biggest problems in society is the breakdown of the traditional two-parent family. A child who doesn't know his own father is like a rudderless ship lost at sea, tossed to and fro by the waves and unable to chart a course home.

But dads don't only have the responsibility to be earthly role models to their kids. Children get their impression of God primarily through the impression they have of their father.

If a dad is a demanding taskmaster who's never satisfied, then his kids will grow up thinking they'll never be able to please God, either. If dad's a slack disciplinarian, his kids will think he's a pushover; then when they grow into adulthood, they'll think they can get away with anything without facing the consequences of their actions. An absentee father fosters the image of a God who doesn't care or, worse yet, is dead.

Charles Stanley pastors Atlanta's First Baptist Church. His popular radio and television program, "In Touch," appears throughout the US as well as in many foreign countries. In his book, *How To Listen To God*, he recounts a story of a young man who told him, "When I come before God to pray, I get the same withering feeling as when I talk to my father. It's as if I see my father when I talk to God."

I recently attended a fund-raiser for a crisis pregnancy center. After dinner that evening, a young woman shared her story of unwed motherhood. "My life was shattered," she said tearfully after learning she was pregnant. "How was I going to face my family, my friends, and my church?"

Being distraught, she contemplated suicide. Finally, she told her parents. As she looked up at her father, expecting condemnation, she saw unconditional love in his face. "After that, I started looking at my heavenly Father in a different light," she said.

Here was a dad who realized the awesome responsibility he had to his daughter to love her and be a godly example in her life. As they embraced, I am sure she felt his love and compassion. Their encounter that day was as if this young woman had looked God himself in the face.

The apostle Paul wrote, "Fathers, do not provoke your children, lest they become discouraged." On this Father's Day, that's especially good advice to all of us dads.

A Clacking Tongue

By Eileen Key

In our technological, sound-bite age, words are often spoken without thought of impending consequences. Ask the errant newscaster or coach who belittles a team and earns scorn. Eating crow is unpleasant. And asking for forgiveness is hard. My father illustrated that point in a way I'll never forget.

"But, Daddy, she is a bad girl. Everyone at school talks about her."

My father's wrinkled forehead, lifted eyebrow, and stern brown eyes bore into my baby blues.

"Daddy, even Mary Ann and Cindy say that Linda is a bad girl," I whined.

A cold silence continued on his part.

I shrank in my chair, my twelve-year-old short legs dangling. "I won't apologize."

Daddy stood up and left the room, pipe tobacco wafting behind him.

The previous day, I had joined in gossip about a friend. The friend's mother overheard and called my father. Now, I was paying the piper. Daddy said I had to apologize to Mrs. Reed and to Linda. My reality screamed, "Unfair." But, truth was, I knew he was right.

My pharmacist father seldom had to use physical force to mete out punishment. His demeanor was enough to cast me into remorse. I knew I would apologize.

Just before dinner, Daddy appeared in the doorway.

"Get your shoes on. We're going to see Mrs. Reed." He spun on his heel before I could utter a word. Reluctantly, I laced my saddle-oxfords and met him in the den. We drove down West 43rd Street in silence. A cold knot settled in the pit of my stomach. I cast angry glances in Daddy's direction, yet his eyes never left the road.

As we pulled into the Reed's driveway, I felt nauseous. "Daddy, I think I'm going to be sick."

"You'll be fine." He got out of the car and waited for me.

I clambered from the front seat and trudged toward the front door. Mrs. Reed met us at the first knock. I peeked around her massive frame and saw Linda seated on their sofa, tears running down her cheeks. Shame washed through me. Without thinking, I dashed to my friend and hugged her.

"I'm sorry, Linda. I shouldn't have said something mean about you. I'm so sorry." My tears mingled with hers. When Mrs. Reed approached us, I spoke the same words.

Linda sniffled, "I thought you were my friend."

Humiliated, I cried, "I am. I am your friend. Those girls were talking, and I wanted them to like me. I just said what they did. But they don't really know you. I'm sorry. I should never have said what I did. Will you forgive me?"

Our twelve-year-old hearts melded together through our tears. Mrs. Reed's admonishment stung when she stated she thought better of me. A raw painful tearing began in my soul.

Daddy leaned against the door frame and gave us a few minutes to chat. Finally, he pushed off and said we needed to leave for dinner. He thanked Mrs. Reed for seeing us, and we left.

Clambering into our '59 Chevy, my tearstained cheeks cooled by the breeze, I waited for Daddy's lecture. He drove home, nary a word spoken. I watched the familiar streets flash by until we pulled into our driveway.

Shifting into park, Daddy turned in the seat and said, "I'm proud of you." He slid from the car and walked into the house.

Proud of me? I'd been gossiping, rude, vindictive, and he was proud of me? I mulled over the events of the past hour. What had made my father proud? I needed to know.

I scampered into the den, the smell of Prince Albert tobacco and spaghetti mingling in the air. I sidled up to the recliner, perched on the arm of the chair, and leaned against Daddy's side. "Why are you proud of me?"

"Eileen, today you learned a valuable life lesson. You saw for yourself how gossip spreads, and how painful it is to another person. Your tongue can be a great tool or a great enemy, and only you can control it. When you witnessed firsthand what you'd done, you didn't need any prompting from me to know what to say. You were wise enough to ask for forgiveness;

to admit you were wrong. That takes courage. I'm proud of you for your courageous actions tonight."

I slid from the chair and was enveloped in a tobacco-hazed hug. I retreated to my bedroom and my childish world a little wiser.

That day is imprinted upon my soul, into my very being. It is one of the pillars of my integrity. I learned, without a doubt, a life-lesson which has served me well. The tongue is a mighty sword, and it is a daily struggle to keep it under control.

"Failure is success if we learn from it."

– Malcomb S. Forbes

Just Four Words

By Mary Lou Healy

My father descended from a long line of thrifty, hard-working Yankee farmers. He was a quiet man, sparing of speech, not tall, but a square block of strength, shaped by years of physical labor. Like another Yankee, Calvin Coolidge, he spoke only when he had something to say and otherwise, was silent.

Dad wasn't big on giving advice but I learned a lot just by listening and observing him at work and in his dealings with other men. He was a shrewd bargainer but always honest and fair. I've watched him in the long hours: up before dawn, working after sunset under floodlights in the farmyard and as he packed his truck with peaches and corn for the 4 a.m. drive to the Boston wholesale market.

He hadn't always been a farmer. He didn't especially like the work and particularly detested cows in their bovine slowness and recalcitrance. Yet, when Grandpa became ill—a long, agonizing journey toward death—Dad returned to the family farm to "take up the slack." Duty was never mentioned. It was just something you did, willingly and with love.

When I once asked him what would be the best way to handle whatever life threw at me, he didn't even have to think twice. His answer summed it all up for me in the context he knew best.

"Plow a straight furrow!" he replied.

When In Doubt

By Anne Abernathy Roth

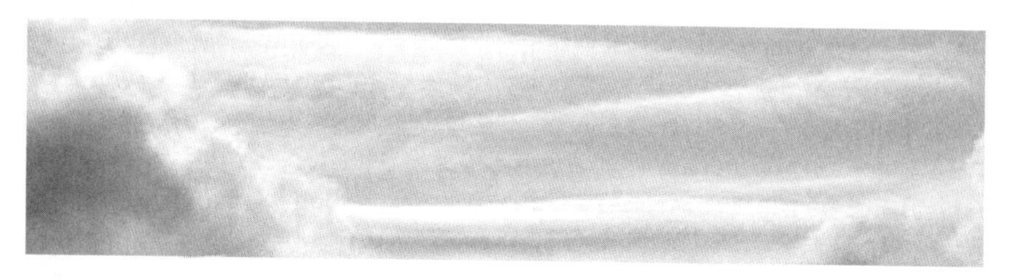

My father passed away over twenty years ago, but his words still echo today reminding me to always proceed with caution. *"When in doubt...don't,"* the phrase that he reinforced so often to me as a child, I continue to apply to my life on a regular basis. Whenever I am faced with a decision, whether big or small, I remember his guiding words. And, if I have any hesitation in my mind, I stop and think about his advice and wait until I can make a clear, informed decision.

His fatherly advice still applies to almost everything I incur in everyday life as an adult. If I am out shopping for a new dress and I can't decide whether it looks good on me from all angles or whether the fabric is the ideal weight, I pause to reconsider. If I continue to wonder if the style is age appropriate or the quality is worth the asking price, upon hesitating, once again I remember his words of wisdom. Obviously, there is doubt floating through my mind about making the purchase, so, in heeding his words, I don't buy it.

If my teenage son asks to borrow my car to go out with some friends, as a concerned parent I think before responding to his question. After checking the current weather conditions, envisioning an unskilled driver on slick, icy roads, and realizing the possible consequences, I naturally hesitate to think before answering him. Always between my thoughts and my final answer wriggles my father's repetitive words, *"When in doubt ...don't."* Therefore, with doubt currently overloading my parental brain circuits, I say "no" to my son. His grandfather smiles from above.

After retrieving sliced ham from the refrigerator, smelling the package, and checking the color to determine if I should discard it or not, I recall his quote and quickly pitch the ham into the trash. Why would I check the color and smell if there was no lingering doubt? I would not. Therefore, the fact that I even considered serving the meat proved that I had doubts concerning freshness. If I had not adhered to my internal warning, my family may have taken ill. An ounce of prevention is worth a pound of cure. Luckily, my father taught me that lesson as well.

His lesson of caution still applies to my decisions in the many years since I last heard his voice. My father taught me many other useful guidelines, but this particular quote of his remains in my mind to protect me. The words are useful. The concept is smart. The application of the words to my decision making process has often protected me from making major mistakes. His four simple words repeated over and over again have proven to change outcomes and prevent wrongful decisions.

Jurors are asked to render a guilty verdict only if there is no "unreasonable doubt." My father taught me that if you hold any doubt in your mind when deciding about something—anything at all, just wait. Don't act. Don't react. Don't do anything. Do not decide until you have acquired enough time to obtain your answer based upon current, accurate, logical information that has been gathered and sorted with a clear open mind. Then, if guided by good judgment from past circumstances, and if there is absolutely no doubt at all lingering in the back of your mind, decide. But, if there is even a *hint* of doubt remaining—don't. Just wait. Proceed with caution. My father who is in heaven will be proud of you.

Patience by Example

By Sharon C. McGonigal

My father, who spoke few words to each of us twelve children, did impart some gems of wisdom to live by when he spoke directly to us, the general audience. On one occasion, when I was an adult, I had an opportunity to talk to him, one on one, as he drove me to a job interview. Advice was not discussed while we drove; we talked about road conditions and the people who had settled in the area. As I look back and search for those pieces of advice he gave me I realized that the most important lessons I learned from him were not by him telling me directly, but through his example. The information he told us directly was important.

He directly told us, never stand with your hands in your pocket for a few reasons. You could get mugged, you could slip and fall and land on your face; and in the work world if there is work to be done you'll look lazy to an employer. Consequently I don't stand around with my hands in my pockets and if I see my children standing that way, I tell them my father's words.

In passing he'd say things like, "If you jog with heavy army boots on, when it comes time for sprinting in a race you'll fly like the wind." When delays happened, he would whistle or hum a tune. He didn't complain and he never said he was bored. What he thought of? I don't know. His thoughts must have been positive, because he would respond happily when he was addressed; I regret not asking his thoughts.

At the lake, our family retreat, he would teach us how to observe and look for unusual things. He'd go for a walk around the lake properties, checking the neighbors' cabins, telling us he was walking the trap line.

Afterward he'd tell us who was around, if there was new damage in the area, a downed tree or a dead porcupine, and if anyone's cabin had been broken into.

Around the campfire, he'd point out a bird, the camp robber, and tell us to observe and watch its habits. He'd throw a crumb out and tell us that they'll swoop in at you and take it right from your hand. In the spring, he would watch the ice break-up. We'd stand with him to listen to the wind blow, the ice moan and then watch it crumple against the shore. On drives to the lake if a coyote crossed the road he would slow down and say "watch, as soon as the coyote is on the other side it'll turn around and look over its shoulder." Sure enough, it did.

Near the end of his time he started reading old encyclopedias and he'd come searching for us; he'd say, "Listen to this…." Then he'd read a passage, chuckle, go sit and continue reading. To this day, that time has instilled in me the excitement over discovering new bits of information.

Another lesson he taught us was to pay attention to detail. While driving he said, "Know all the bends in the road and always look back to see what the view is for when you have to make a return trip; especially if it is at night, you'll know what it looks like and you won't get lost."

At the lake, he told us, "Listen to the sounds of the vehicles driving in; know who's driving so you can get off the road. It could mean life or death." For my dad, he learned and lived that in World War II; he needed to know the path he had traveled, the sound of an enemy vehicle approaching, whether it was by land or by air, and its speed. For him it was a life or death situation.

Back then it seemed silly. "It could mean life or death" sounded ominous to us children, but it really isn't so silly when you think of today's traffic on the road. If you listen for vehicles as you drive or cross the road then you can predict the state of the driver, if they are speeding or not. So, I tell my children to listen for vehicles coming from behind when crossing the road; it could save their life.

One important lesson that he didn't comment on, but I absorbed by example, was his driving habits. He didn't yell at other drivers on the road and he never had any traffic violations—speeding tickets or collisions. He could boast he had a clean driving record, but he didn't. Road rage and driving impaired was not part of his vocabulary while he was alive. Through that kind of an example I've made a commitment to drive my dad's way. For me it costs nothing to drive that way; and I have peace of mind, that at the end of the day, I didn't cause any roadway harm nor did I yell at anyone.

All of those lessons hinged on what I consider his most important life's lesson—something he did not formally communicate, but demonstrated daily—his patience. He did not openly announce, "I am a patient man." He just lived it. Delays happened, he'd hum a tune and observe. Today living in the undercurrents of a rushed society, road rage, desk rage, rush-hour traffic backed up for hours, I remember my father's patience.

On our weekly grocery-shopping day, he'd sit in the station wagon on a hot summer day with the window rolled down humming a tune. Our vehicle was not air-conditioned and shopping took hours. During winter, he'd bundle up and walk around the vehicle a few times to stay warm. He did this while he waited for my mother. A couple of the older children went in with her and a couple of the younger ones stayed with him. I was in the younger category. As time passed he never swore or clock watched. He would comment on the vehicles or people that went by. A shame I never did ask what he was thinking while waiting.

When she wheeled out two carts of groceries a couple of hours later, he'd step out of the station wagon, and load the bags of groceries for her while she got in on the passenger's side and the other kids piled in. Not once did he complain over how long it took nor how much money it cost. When we arrived home he would unload the groceries with the children then sit and fold the paper bags. For as long as I could remember, he drove her to wherever she needed to go because my mom did not have a driver's license. Each time he did, he waited patiently.

His patience saved him his life. My cousin in Ireland recently related a story to us about how my father came under heavy enemy fire in the battlefield. "He took cover in a crater. In doing so he became conscious of something 'digging' into his side; while it was uncomfortable, it was not unbearable. He remained in this position until it was safe to move." His thoughts turned to finding out what was poking him when he got out. The enemy fire dissolved around him and when it was safe "he put his hand down to remove whatever was 'digging' into him and uncovered a crucifix."

My cousin continued the story; "All around your father, his comrades were either badly wounded or dead; your father was totally unscathed." Growing up, my father never told us this story; my cousin sent the crucifix and the story to my oldest sister, which she sent me a copy of. Waiting out enemy fire and being uncomfortable while waiting became clear for me the extent of his tolerance level and patience.

I now single-parent five children, and when I'm uncomfortable and faced with line-ups in grocery stores, angry-sounding people or traffic backed up for miles, I hum an Irish tune—to remind me of my father. I observe the goings on around me and I write stories in my head. I use my ears to listen to the different sounds in the building.

When I'm with my children, I tell them what their grandfather would do in those situations if he stood here. In a long grocery line-up I tell the kids to write a story in their heads. If they mention the words, "I'm bored" I put them to work and tell them, not with their hands in their pockets. Out walking, I'll hold them back on a trail and tell them to listen for the sounds and observe the details around them and I hope I show them the same amount of patience my father demonstrated daily. Looking back, all the advice he imparted was immersed in patience; one he didn't know he set by example.

Don't Be Sorry

By Susan DeWolfe

"You know," my boss said, "we are hard pressed to keep trained and experienced managers. That's why I wanted to speak with you about your decision to retire. We are in a position to offer you a wonderful opportunity. You can keep quiet about your decision to retire, take thirty days off, and come back to work and draw both your retirement and your salary at the same time. You don't have to give me an answer today, but I need to know before you submit your retirement paperwork to personnel. Take some time and think it over. Just let me know first."

"Thanks," I said.

I knew, of course, about the opportunity before she told me. The agency had put it in writing and sent it out over the interoffice email. In a high stress environment, we lost staff at the rate of about twenty-eight percent a year. Managers were always training new people, monitoring them, and trying to find ways to help them succeed and stay. The best ones stayed long enough to promote into management. The ones who couldn't do the work successfully or who really hated the job were encouraged to resign and work in a less demanding venue. Everyone else who stayed had a reason.

For some, it was doing a job that was needed and making a difference in the lives of the families we served. For some, it was economic necessity. For some, work in a crisis intervention agency was exciting, and other work seemed boring in comparison. For some, it was the training opportunities the agency provided. We were always learning something new.

For me, it had been a combination of all of those things. I loved making a difference. It was exciting. I did learn new things all the time. And with two children still in college, we could certainly use the additional income.

But I had come to realize that the job was so all-enveloping that there was nothing else. My family seldom saw me before eight or nine at night. It was not uncommon for me to work until after midnight. My life long dreams of other opportunities postponed "until there was more time" remained unrealized. Still, an increase of almost half my salary for the same work I was already doing was incredibly tempting. No student loans for the girls. The house paid off early. More financial security for the family.

I asked the administrative assistant to take calls for me, and walked down the Strand for a cup of coffee and some time to think. The tour ship was in dock and her passengers crowded the tourist district. On the corner, a guitarist played jazz beside his open case, and horse drawn carriages clopped down the street. The Galveston sky was a blinding blue, and the wind whispered between the historic buildings of the spring street—truly a Chamber of Commerce sort of day. I was wool gathering, stepping down one of Galveston's flood-avoiding three-foot curbs, when the memory came; vivid as the morning sky.

Dad had been gone for over fifteen years. But even in memory, his piercing brown eyes commanded my attention. "You have a decision to make," he had said my sophomore year in college. "Nobody can make it for you. You know what is at stake, and some possible rewards and consequences. Here is the thing I want you to remember: If you are going to be sorry for something you do, don't do it. But if you have made up your mind to do it, don't be sorry."

What an incredible gift! In that short statement, Dad set me free to be my own person; to make my own decisions, and finally, to know that having weighed the options and made a decision, I could go forward without regrets.

The sharp tang of coffee on the morning air called me into a shop to take a break and ponder my decision. Whatever I decided, I knew I wouldn't regret it.

Thanks, Dad. I miss you every day.

Words of Wisdom

By Mike Marinaro

My dad passed away nearly thirty years ago but I can still remember his words of wisdom like it was only yesterday. I am so glad we had a good relationship and I consider myself very lucky to have had such a wonderful dad.

The one thing that sticks in my mind the most and has helped me to make so many decisions in my life was a simple phrase from my dad. He used to always tell me, "If you wouldn't want to do it in front of me and your mother, then you shouldn't be doing it at all!"

Those words echoed in my mind many times as a teenager and really did keep me out of trouble. Some of the people I hung out with were not of the best character and tended to make poor decisions. However, whenever I was tempted to do something bad I remembered my father's words and usually made the right choice. I'm not saying I was an angel (I did get into my share of trouble as most teenagers do), but I was fortunate to have my father as a good role model to look up to. His words helped me do the right thing so many times!

I can recall one time in particular where three of my friends were getting ready to break into a house and vandalize it just for the fun of it. They wanted me to come along with them, but I thought about my mom and dad watching me. And I knew I wouldn't want them to see me doing that! Of course my friends called me chicken and made fun of me, but I remained strong and walked away with my head held high! A few years later those same three friends of mine ended up in prison for robbing a store at gunpoint! Thanks Dad for those words of wisdom.

Another incident from my teenage years where my dad's advice taught me a valuable lesson involved a freight train. We lived near railroad tracks and used to always hop on the box cars and take rides. This was great fun but very dangerous. After a few rides I realized that my mom and dad would be horrified if they could see their son running along beside a moving train and trying to jump on. I decided that my dad was right again and stayed away from the tracks. Not too long after that one of my friends was playing around on top of a box car and accidentally touched a live wire, he was electrocuted and nearly died. He survived but ended up with bad burns and lost a leg. He now has a wooden leg and terrible scars all over his body. Once again my father's advice had been worth following.

Now I have four children and six grandchildren and I often find myself repeating those very words to them. In fact, even today I still think about Dad's advice when I face tempting situations. My mom and dad are both gone now, but I'm sure they are sitting in Heaven watching me. They can be proud to know that I followed Dad's advice and they won't see me doing anything that they would be ashamed of.

"Man's mind once stretched by a new idea, never regains its original dimension."

– Oliver Wendell Holmes

Where We Are

By Annie Shapero

When a parent dies, it's terribly easy to drown in the empty space you're left with. At first I felt amputated, an integral piece of me was missing, and I no longer knew how or where to walk with no one to guide me, or carry me when my own legs were tired. Miraculously my father's death pushed me to fill the void, to live beyond the supposed confines of myself and to fuse with world around me. Perhaps the greatest lesson my father instilled in me, was to appreciate and participate in every aspect of our wondrous existence. Only when we are wholly part of the world, can we know what is just, and act accordingly.

I was living in Italy when I got the news. It hit like a sniper's bullet, a complete shock, and thrust me into yet another foreign place, some uncharted territory of the globe. I refused to believe it then, and sometimes still it seems impossible. I hadn't seen my dad for several months, and struggling to recall our last hurried words on the telephone, I felt awash in guilt for being so far away.

The day after, I awoke to luminous morning sunshine streaming in my window and I knew my father wouldn't have wanted me to be in any other place. With heightened senses and nerves on overdrive, I walked through the sun-warmed streets, conscious of every aspect of my existence: heels click-clacking on cobblestones, hair brushing my cheeks, and the still-chilled breeze of the previous evening against my bare shoulders. I walked for several hours, pausing in my favorite spots of the city and I took my father with me. I stopped under Garibaldi Bridge. Where I sat on a broken pilaster and gazed at a jutting cement block that sliced the smooth flow of the river like the helm of a ship. It was a place to reflect, and with the waves of the Tiber rushing past, I knew I could only go forward.

He had never been to visit me, only lived my experience through emails and enthusiastic phone calls. While he often reminded me to check my finances and stay serious about my studies, his voice was warm and almost envious. He always had something to add to my itinerary. There were wines to sample, and of course visits to their regions of origin. He was as passionate about wine as he was about life, and taught me to appreciate its color, fragrance, and flavor, but most of all, its story.

There was La Scala Opera House in Milan, a five-hour train ride from Rome, but well worth it, he said. I grew up with opera blasting from the basement, where my father would lose himself to the strains of Puccini, Verdi, and Rossini. He taught me the stories of every opera, and what the foreign phrases meant. For my father, music was not a pleasure reserved for the ears, but the door to a multi-sensorial experience. Opera, especially, was to be explored, lived, and loved.

There were the hot springs in the Tuscan hillsides, which he had never visited, but had longed to, as the simple beauty of the landscape and the miracle of its existence fascinated him. "Just imagine, Annie, pure boiling water bursting through the surface of the earth!" he would exclaim, following with geological explanations, involving volcanoes and the center of the earth, which I ignored at the time as all children do, spouting automatically, "I know, I know," admitting later however, that it was remarkable.

For my father, the world was meant to be explored and studied. He planted lilies in the backyard, many varieties hailing from different countries he'd visited. So awed by their splendor, he had researched and ordered them specifically for our garden. He explained in detail when to watch for them, and how to care for the delicate bulbs so they would return each summer.

The world was wildly beautiful in my father's eyes. His letters were packed with adjectives describing sunsets, sonatas, the lake at dawn, or a book I ought to read. He dove beyond the mere esthetic qualities of things, seeking to understand where they came from, or what they could teach us.

He encouraged me to move to Italy for a while, to cultivate my appreciation for a culture different from my own and to discover all of its astounding artistic, culinary, musical, and architectural creations. He taught me to savor the real pleasures of life; they are multitudinous if we know how to see and feel. He encouraged me to truly know as many people as possible, to build relationships, and make life-long friends. He explained that deep affection between two people never dies and that you can love more than once in a lifetime. He taught me to always think for myself, to be aware of my position, and to approach every decision not only with clarity and rationality, but also with sensitivity and an appreciation for the real joy of living.

Recently during a trip to the Tuscan hot springs of Saturnia, I sat in the hot bubbling water with a friend and chatted away about my dad and how much he would have loved it there. My friend looked me in the eye and said, "Your father is in everything you are; he's with you all the time." I burst into tears as he hugged me, telling me it was normal; I missed him after all.

I feel it's more than missing him, however. I do of course, every single day. But when something new and fascinating happens to me, I feel him. When I am awed to silence or overcome with tears over something as simple as a song on the radio, I recall moments spent together, hand in hand, admiring the autumn leaves for their brilliant colors, and he is telling me why they are so. We listen to Beethoven's *Fifth Symphony*, incredulous that a deaf man could compose such a masterpiece.

Learning and loving the world was everything to my father. We used to watch Barbra Streisand's film, *Yentl*, and he would explain that her story was also the story of my ancestors. For a child it was simply nice music, and I would cry every time she lit a candle for her father and sang to the stars. Today the film has a far greater meaning. It is my story as well, as I seek to live to the fullest, taking in every detail with my eyes, my ears, and my heart. I marvel at all things beautiful and wondrous, and listen to those who can teach me something.

I thank my father for instilling in me a willingness to study and understand all aspects of the world, while realizing what a wonderful creation surrounds us. And I know that while we may never know the secrets of the universe, knowing ourselves and where we are, makes us incredibly human, and guides us as we walk through life, never truly alone.

Life Deals Some Bitter Pills

By Colleen Tillger

As a sixteen year old girl, I had my heart broken. It wasn't anything extraordinary, just your typical "first true love." Danny and I had been dating for about six months and I just knew that we were going to be together forever.

My parents had divorced four years earlier and I was living with my father. Just the two of us. Whenever I think over the different stages of my life, the time I spent living with my dad always stands out as the most peaceful. My father and I shared a close bond unusual for a teenage girl and her dad. We did lots of stuff together and even had fun grocery shopping.

I was slumped on the couch in a teary daze when my father walked in after work the day Danny dumped me. The apartment was silent; no TV, no radio, just the sound of my sniffles and sobs. Dad immediately recognized something was wrong and sat down beside me.

"What's the matter, sweetheart?" he asked.

"Danny broke up with me!"

He put his arm around me and pulled me close so I could rest my head on his shoulder. Patting my arm he asked awkwardly if there was anything he could do. I shook my head and sniffed loudly.

"Can I just go to Stacy's?"

Stacy was my best friend and I needed her comfort and sarcastic wit. She could always make me laugh even when I felt horrible.

"Sure, sweetheart. Just be home by ten."

Ten o'clock was my curfew on a weeknight. I could stay out until midnight on the weekends if Dad knew where I was, and sometimes later if I had a good reason. He was always very democratic with me and we discussed every rule that was made, changed, or bent. Dad really trusted me. He always told me that I was a very intelligent girl and he knew I'd make the right decisions.

I spent that evening at Stacy's house, where I cried a lot and called Danny lots of nasty names. We had mean conversations about him and talked about all his annoying qualities. Stacy's older brothers offered to beat him up for me, which I declined. Walking home, I felt a lot better, but still had a dumbbell in the pit of my stomach.

I opened our apartment door at 9:45 and shuffled into the kitchen. The light was on and Dad was sitting at the table reading the newspaper and drinking coffee as he always did in the evenings. With my head down, I plopped into a chair and he folded his paper, placing it gently on the table beside the steaming mug.

I looked up and saw a box on the table, the kind you get from the bakery at the grocery store. Leaning against the box was a greeting card envelope with my name written on it in my dad's scratchy handwriting.

He cleared his throat and gestured toward the box. "I, uh, got you a pie."

I stared at the box and read the label. It was a Boston Crème pie, my favorite. I looked up at my dad and he smiled slightly, hopefully. I took the card away from the box and pulled it out of the envelope. It was one of those "I know you're going through a rough time" cards. Inside it, he wrote that he just wants to try and keep my spirit high. A "p.s." at the bottom noted, "What do you think of this neat environmental card?"

I couldn't help but smile as I read the environmentally correct card made from recycled paper and the silly postscript. My dad was such a sappy, mushy dad and I loved him for that. Dad was smiling wider when I looked up at him with happier tears in my eyes. The look of my father's deep, sincere caring warmed his cheeks and I knew that no boy I might fall in love with could ever compete.

He cleared his throat again and said, "So let's cut this thing, huh?"

We set out paper plates and forks and Dad cut the pie into large gooey slices. He filled a mug with coffee, set it down in front of me, and I knew that he expected us to stay up for a while. We stayed up past midnight that night and he just let me talk about Danny. He wasn't judgmental at all (he never was), he didn't trivialize my feelings like some parents would when their teenager got dumped (oh, just get over it, some might say), he really *listened* to me. And I felt safe, comforted, loved.

He only offered one piece of advice and I never forgot it. Even today, almost fifteen years later, I can hear his voice crystal clear: "Life deals lots of bitter pills, sweetheart. But they go down easier if you just swallow them whole. If you hold 'em in your mouth or chew 'em up, they taste really nasty, just like aspirin."

Now, at the time, I was a little confused by this analogy and just let it go as another of my dad's weird pieces of wisdom. But over the years I thought of those words a lot and drew on their deeper meaning. Whenever life dealt me a "bitter pill" I remembered my dad's words, and the day he died, I clung to them.

My dad died fairly young, he was only 54 and I was 24. It was sudden, unexpected, and I felt completely destroyed. I needed those words then more than I ever had. Dad knew I was strong. He knew that I could take life's "bitter pills" and go on. Dad always knew these things and that gave me the courage to believe them myself.

I kept that "neat, environmental card" and I am so glad. After he died, I pulled it out and read the words again for the first time since I was that sixteen year old girl. It said "This stressful time won't last forever—please believe in yourself as I believe in you. And remember that each tomorrow is a whole new opportunity to begin again, to live again, and to be happy. Take care of yourself."

My father's comfort came down from heaven and wrapped me in warmth as I read that card. The day my father died, life dealt me the most bitter pill of all. And I swallowed it. I swallowed that bitter, painful, lump of a pill and believed in myself as I held his memory close and moved forward.

I have had some great successes, some great failures, some great heartbreaks, and some great disappointments in my life since my father died. And with each bitter pill life has dealt, I have drawn on his wisdom to get me through. He taught me to keep moving through the pain, to know that things will get better, to believe in myself and my own ability to heal.

I have shared this story with many people over the years. As long as life keeps dealing those "bitter pills," my father's wisdom is kept alive in the hope and strength it gives to those who are trying to swallow.

As for me, I keep the good times in my heart, the sound of his laughter in my ears, the glint of his smiling eyes in my sight, and his advice in my head. I know he is proud.

Gone But Not Forgotten.... Love Lives On

By Kristy Gillinder

God truly blessed me with wonderful parents. They had a whirlwind courtship, fell deeply in love, and I was the result of their honeymoon. I remember three things about my parents and my father in particular. These three things I have carried with me throughout my entire life. These things I learned from my father have sustained me through some very difficult times in my life.

First, I remember that when my mother walked into the room, my father's face practically lit up. His eyes danced every time he looked at my mother. He obviously loved her with all his heart, and she loved him right back the same way. All of the love he felt for my mother showed on his face. I knew, even as a little girl, that when I was all grown up, I would marry someone who looked at me the same way that my father looked at my mother. And I did. When I met my husband, the first time he looked into my eyes, it reminded me of the exact way my father looked at my mother. And, over the years, my husband still takes my breath away when he looks at me that way, because I know he loves me with all his heart.

The second important lesson I learned from my father was laughter really is the best medicine. I can still hear my parents' laughter and remember their smiling faces. When they laughed and smiled, I knew that everything in the world was okay. I knew that I was safe, protected, and loved. My father's laughter meant that life was good. He had a special way of always looking on the bright side of things. His optimism and love of life was infectious, and it made the lives of those around him better. Today, I still find myself smiling as I recall how my father and mother used to chase each other and giggle like two mischievous kids. Their merriment made me happy and they never failed to include me in it.

The third important teaching from my father was that when you love someone, you will willingly lay down your life for them. When I was five years old, the ultimate tragedy struck my family. My parents died in a horrific accident that I witnessed. My father could have escaped, but he went back, without hesitating, to save my mother. Their accident occurred on a boat. My mother was not a strong swimmer. She was entangled and trying to get out, and my father died trying to save her. I was completely devastated to lose the two most important people in my life, especially at such a young age. However, looking back on it now, I would have expected nothing less from my father. He loved my mother so much that he never thought of his own safety. All he wanted was to save her life, and he gave his trying to do so. And I know, without a doubt, that I would do the same thing for my family.

While I ache sometimes when I think of my parents, I always remember the good times. How I wish they were here to meet my beloved husband and my precious children. My faith in God reminds me that we will all be together again someday. Until then, I do my best to honor them every day. I especially want to take the lessons I learned from my father to heart and be the same kind of person he was. If I succeed in doing this, then I will be the same kind of example for my children that my father was for me.

Old Spice

By Nancy Robinson

Eager to pose words that resonate, I consider why I write. Pencil to paper soothes me, but passion alone is little inspiration. I think that I write for my dead father because he cannot tell me stories anymore.

A hopeless romantic, Dad was sure that only because of goodness did the sun rise everyday and that in each day goodness could be found. An opinionated raconteur, the gift of storytelling was his greatest legacy. Culled from interesting work days, he relayed adventures brimming with colorful characters and engaging plots.

Transformation from dusty to dapper came easily for Dad who worked 16-hour days absorbing heat and greasy odors that filled restaurant kitchens where he honed his craft. Messy work but pleasurable for him. He liked that which was laborious and tangible. His bruised and burned hands bore cuts bequeathed to him by the knives he wielded as a chef. Each wound had a story. Stories he seemed to always tell.

Emerging from his room in a freshly pressed double-breasted olive green suit, elegantly draped over a crisp white shirt adorned with one of his many Father's Day ties, Dad's shoes were polished, his nails neatly clipped and trimmed. The strong scent of Old Spice emanated from his olive-beige, freshly shaven skin. Pieces of tissue paper were anchored to bloody spots where his heavy, arthritic-ridden hand, while manipulating a razor, tore skin off his face.

"Where are you going, Daddy?"

"I'm going to surprise Mommy and take her out to dinner. She'll be home from work soon. Let me know when you hear the garage."

"Okay, I will. By the way, Daddy, you look nice."

"Thank you, Charlie."

That's what he called me—Charlie. Not my name, but a moniker used to encompass my multifaceted self. A petite, underweight little girl with long, frizzy braids and knobby knees, I had a decisively pointy chin only overwhelmed by the nose that was too big for my face. And I was a tomboy who needed a tomboy name. During those years, while growing into myself, I relished climbing trees, making mud pies, and shadowing my father as he made repairs around the house. I listened to his stories, which became windows to my world. He appreciated the interest since everyone else seemed eager to avoid him when the storytelling mood struck. I was fascinated with his tales, and with the advent of my special name we became collaborators on the greatest stories ever told between father and daughter.

The creaky, off-the-track clamor made by the garage door was familiar. A repair my father never made, it was a signal to us kids that one of our parents was home.

"Mommy's home, Daddy."

"Okay, merci."

Merci. Probably the only French word my father spoke to me since he—an immigrant and Haitian exile—was directed by Catholic Nuns not to speak his native tongue to his children, lest it "do them irreparable harm." My parents only wanted to do the right thing, you understand. Their Catholic Church spelled out for them what "right" was, and like good Catholics, they avoided dissension. In the ruins of conformity we were robbed of our heritage and culture.

Memories embitter as I remember being asked questions as a child.

"Do you speak French, like your parents?"

"No."

I am ashamed and feel cheated of what was inherently mine.

Eventually I studied it and excelled at twirling the foreign words around my tongue. Classmates wondered if I held unfair advantage, with my parents being from a French-speaking country and all. It offered me little advantage except perhaps for the intrinsically passionate zeal with which I became devoted to the language that I was taught by Roman Catholic nuns, sisters of those responsible for denying it to me in the first place. *Quelle ironie*.

I always loved a good anecdote and Dad was a great teller of tales. Often spewed over aromas of sausage and peppers or his famously delicious Steak Diane, the scent of Old Spice after-shave still oozing from his well-worn face, others thought him a chatterbox and they avoided his storytelling sessions. Through my father and his talkative way, I learned the value of vivid characters that jump out at you from a story, close enough to touch and smell. It was the creative way in which he made me curious about life's machinations.

Though at times it seemed like he never stopped talking, he did. And when not telling a story, Dad could be found reading one. Books, magazines and newspapers were key references he used. I wondered what in the world he found so interesting all the time. I wondered and wondered until my own curiosity encouraged me to become a voracious reader. I consumed Poe, Baldwin, Dickinson and Camus. Reading became the perfect extracurricular activity for me because I could do it alone—the perfect venue for an introvert. Reading aloud while alone in my room, I discovered my own voice. Soon, reading was not enough to satisfy my literary palate. I joined the Speech Club in high school, traveling the region competing with trophy-winning readings of my favorite works. My shyness overcome, I became a public speaker. Reading enjoyed, speaking accomplished, and writing was the natural next step to learning to become who I really am. Now I do it everyday, spewing stories and recounting tales.

Through lessons my father taught me, I've come to believe that there is always a colorful way to say something, just as there is always something to be said—even in the absence of my favorite storyteller. My father died dedicated to his family. And although he had no fortune to leave his eight children, his bequest of stories and love of literature stood strong and fast. Dependable as the rising sun, a day never passed without a good story from Dad. It made me feel mysterious and theatrical. Sometimes, I even felt like a character in one of his tales, especially when he called me Charlie. Now, Charlie tells stories of her own.

"The ultimate measure of a man is not where he stands in moments of comfort and convenience, but where he stands at times of challenge and controversy."

– Martin Luther King, Jr.

The Day I Wasn't an All-Star

By Dan Markham

In the early summer of 1979, all I wanted was to be an All-Star.

I played shortstop on my Little League team in the Town of Cortland. The season was winding down and the league's coaches were getting ready to vote on the twelve team representatives. I prayed that I would be included.

I was then, as I am now, a baseball junkie. I spent most of the daylight hours playing ball, whether organized league play, sandlot games with friends, or alone, by tossing a ball against my cousin's steps and fielding the unpredictable bounces that followed.

And as night fell, my bedtime reading consisted of baseball books and magazines of all types. I knew the stats, the teams, the history, and the rules; knowledge that could have been put to good use had the subject been more educational.

My plan had only one problem. I couldn't hit. All that time and energy devoted to the game, and I was still an unimposing figure with a bat in my hands.

Still, I had hope. I was a slick fielder and a good base runner, and maybe, just maybe, that kind of player had a place on a team of big boppers.

Alas, when the coaches convened, they were given one basic instruction: the All-Star team should be comprised of the best hitters. That was the only real consideration, the six skippers were told.

Naturally, it didn't evolve that way. After the obvious selections, politicking took over. Coaches, who doubled as fathers, worked alliances to get their kid a spot on the club.

Surprisingly, I had three of these coaches in my corner. Three guys who didn't care what the rules said. To them, I was an all-star-caliber ballplayer. Four votes were needed for selection. Yet the fourth vote never came. And if you had to finger the culprit behind my exclusion, the only suspect would have been my coach, my father, Peter Markham.

For several rounds of voting, my dad held out on adding me to the team of stars. He reasoned that a team that was supposed to honor the league's best hitters was one that couldn't include me.

But there was a place for Mike Babic, Dad insisted. As my father scanned the list of batting averages, he was dumbfounded by the fact that the kid with the highest average in the league, Babic, had still not been voted onto the team an hour after the selections began.

Several things worked against the first baseman. He wasn't perceived as a great athlete, just a kid who happened to bang out a few extra hits. More importantly, he wasn't a favored son. His parents made no loud noises.

So my dad took up his cause, even though my father couldn't have picked Mike Babic out of a police lineup. He said he was walking out if a vote wasn't taken on Babic during the next round. The other coaches relented, and Mike Babic was an All-Star.

My dad relayed all this to me when he got home. He told me that I would have been on the All-Star team if he had voted for me. But, in his conscience, he knew that I didn't deserve it based on the established qualifications.

It surely couldn't have been easy for him. He wasn't a stern task master, or a man never satisfied with his children's accomplishments. He thought I was a fine ballplayer, and a pretty good kid. He loved me unquestionably, unconditionally, and unabashedly. But under the rules laid out before the meeting, I wasn't an All-Star.

I got over the All-Star snub rather quickly. I was scooped up by an alternate All-Star team, and had a great few weeks playing with them. And I continued playing baseball for years after that, eventually landing a spot on my college team (even though I still couldn't hit).

Yet the lessons I took from my father, my late father, lasted much longer than my baseball career. I discovered that any accolade, no matter how craved, must be earned to be appreciated. To receive an undeserved honor, regardless the reason, was an empty gift. And I learned that you could fight for a cause without any stake in it, as my dad did when he championed the mysterious Mike Babic.

I also discovered that my dad was a man of integrity, and it was a trait he couldn't toss away even to give untold, if temporary, pleasure to a son he truly loved.

But when I look back on that strange night a quarter century ago, one thing stands out above all else. One fact that tells me that my father raised me the right way, from the time I was in diapers to the time I left for college.

When he discussed how the evening had unfolded and my dream had unraveled, as he explained his reasons for leaving me off his ballot, I don't recall ever getting angry. I knew, even in my disappointment, that he had done the right thing. And that's a level of understanding no twelve-year-old boy, not even the slickest of fielders, picks up without excellent coaching.

Consider and Respect Others First

By Patricia P. Miller

Dad was "old school," from the Victorian era when thinking first of others, and only later of yourself, was the guiding principle. His primary lesson, taught early and often, was to think how one's actions impacted others and about first impressions made by one's responses. Consideration and respect were his rules, and beyond that, his behavior modeled these lessons for his children.

He grew up on a farm and knew hard work from the beginning, helping with chores, tending gardens and chickens, learning to handle and love horses. He first rode along in the wagon, and then drove the buggy horse on my grandfather's rural Ohio mail route, learning responsibility and duty at an early age himself. "The mail must go through," was a slogan we heard early and often, and it was applied to life situations far beyond a stamped letter and a smiling picture post card.

Consideration for the rights and feelings of others is the fragrant oil that lubricates and lightens our social and professional interactions. Those who fail to learn this lesson cause friction, hurt, heartache, and disaster as they ricochet through life, trampling on the hearts and souls of those they encounter.

Dad knew better: treat people with consideration and respect, and earn it yourself in return. Leading always by example, he taught us to respect others first.

Working his way out of the small farm town with summer jobs at a pottery and driving spikes on the railroad, he knew how to get ahead. He was the first in his family to leave on the train for college, and earned a lifetime in medicine as the sweet reward.

I remember with a child's sharp focus clearing out the cabin we rented each summer at Lake Hope, the aptly named vacation retreat we all loved. The cabin, a wondrous place made of pine logs, was a simple three-room summer place where I shared a bunk bed with my younger brother, hotly disputing the top bunk rights. The cabin smelled of pine smoke that lingered from the fires crackling in the huge stone fireplace, a memory forever burned in my brain and an instant transport back to those days.

As we pulled sheets from the beds, to place them out on the front stoop for pickup by the cleaning crew, my dad sternly instructed: "Wait! Fold those sheets and towels the way you found them. You want to be asked back, don't you?"

My two brothers and I looked forlornly at the soiled, crumbled pile of linens, and grudgingly began to fold and stack them. Life lesson here: treat the cleanup crew with as much respect as they treated you. Fold the laundry; leave it the way you found it.

"Fold the laundry," and, "The mail must go through," were first instructions of childhood. As we grew and took on more of life's challenges, those lessons played out in ever more complex, demanding situations of teen years and young adulthood. "Be home on time," and, "Do your homework," resonated with, "Look it up yourself," when we whined for assistance with spelling or reference. Do it yourself was another life lesson I applied throughout school and early professional employment, and, Dad was right, doing it yourself with consideration and respect for others was a winner.

My dad has been gone many years now, but his early lessons and inspiration guided me with my own children, too. When they asked for help and I snapped out, "Look it up yourself," I knew Dad was laughing somewhere. When I halted a potential litterbug with a sharp, "Put that in the trash can; don't you want to be asked back," they learned to laugh too, knowing just where that came from.

Leadership from a strong father and critical guidance when needed —which is often quite frequently— are guideposts to a considered, reflective, positive life that shines as a model of respect and consideration for others, ahead of one's self. It's the perfect reflection of the old time Golden Rule, which shines with the same luminosity today and it did then.

Thanks Dad. And yes, I surely do want to be asked back.

A Lesson on Success

By Gail Clanton Diggs

If you were to look in the dictionary and search for a definition for "Daddy's girl," you'd find my name and photograph, I'm sure.

My father was and still is my greatest hero. Both his life and his death taught me how I want to live and how I want to be remembered.

My father was never blessed with perfect health. My memories of him include his battles with high blood pressure and hospital stays. But, through it all, I have no memory of him feeling sorry for himself or blaming anyone for his predicament. I only remember him picking himself up, brushing himself off, thanking God for each new day, and moving on. That's the kind of man he was.

So when his kidneys failed in the fall of 2000, I had no reason to think that this would be anything different. By this time he was in his early seventies, so I knew that he might have a harder time bouncing back than he did during his younger years, but I had no fear that he wouldn't be OK.

And boy was he ever!

Sure, he dreaded going to the dialysis center three times a week. He didn't like the tube that was permanently placed in his arm or the lethargic feeling he was left with when the almost four-hour procedure was over. Yet he endured with a quiet confidence that was the greatest example of leadership, courage and trust in God that I've ever seen.

My father made friends with the staff and fellow clients at the dialysis center and was a source of inspiration to many of them. That's just the kind of man he was.

My father was the kind of man who would gather his family in the car for Sunday afternoon drives to nowhere, and we loved it! We'd ride and ride for hours, singing, laughing, talking, simply enjoying the company of one another.

He was the kind of father who would visit a daughter five hundred miles away in college, "just because"; who never missed a graduation, piano recital, choir concert, school play, church speech, or anything else that included his wife, children, or grandchildren. He could be depended upon to lift your spirits when they were low and reaffirm the value of that one special word: *try*. "If you just try, Gail," he'd tell me, "you might be surprised at all you can accomplish. Never be afraid to try."

You see, with my father I was allowed to dream big, to think highly of myself, and to never doubt that I could do anything I wanted to do. I was his child after all; what more ammunition did I need to take this world by storm!

Being his child was always very special to me. He led by example, and while I certainly wasn't perfect, I never wanted to embarrass or disappoint my father. And that continues to this day, even though I'm a grown woman and he is no longer here on Earth with me.

I still worry about hurting the feelings of others, because that's what my father would do. I still go out of my way to encourage family members, especially the younger ones, because that's what my father would do. And I always take time out of each day to pray, because that's what he would do.

Health complications began to plague my father in the fall of 2003, yet I never imagined that he wouldn't bounce back. He had surgery on October 2nd and doctors told us that everything had gone successfully. Yet on the October 3rd, his earthly vessel passed away.

Now that I look back on that sad, sad time, I realize that maybe, in spite of my father's vessel passing away, everything had, in fact, gone "successfully." My father was able to see his children grown and happy, with homes and families of their own. He held his dignity intact until the end and was surrounded by family and friends who he knew loved him fiercely. And, he had an unwavering faith that allowed him to face life's challenges with the strength of a lion and the grace of a gazelle.

So yes, in a strange, strange way, everything had gone successfully. What a victory!

And because of that victory, my father's presence is still felt on Earth today.

I see him in my mother's calmness, in my brother's values, and in my nephews' wit.

I feel him within me, especially when I begin to feel sad or to doubt myself. I feel him stirring within me, squeezing my hand, encouraging me to keep going.

I hear him telling me to never be afraid to reach for the stars and to always remember what really matters in life—God, family, and friends. The rest is, as the popular book series says, just "stuff."

The memories of my beloved father will remain within me forever. He left for me a clear path to follow that will help ensure that I grab hold of and appreciate all that life has to offer; that I treat people kindly, laugh heartily, and that I never forget to pray.

By example, my father showed me how to live, and how to die, "successfully." And for this I am eternally grateful.

A Love Letter to My Dad on Father's Day

By Michele H. Lacina

A lot will be written about fathers and sons on Father's Day. Overlooked is the special relationship between a father and his daughter.

Sociologists and psychologists believe that women learn a great deal by studying the role model of the male in a family. When choosing a mate, women compare the men they date to see how they measure up to the father figure they interacted with while growing up.

Now that I've crossed the half-century mark, I see how much I learned from my father. Here are five simple lessons he taught me that all of us would do well to remember every Father's Day.

1. Your word is your bond.

Many people who attended my father's funeral remarked that he was a man of honor. Over and over, I heard: "You always knew where you stood with Sonny," or "He kept his word. He treated everyone fairly."

Honor is a missing standard nowadays. We've elevated greed at the expense of this longtime friend. Money comes and goes—what remains in life are memories. How you are perceived after death is your legacy.

2. Education is never wasted.

At eighteen I found a man I loved and was sure I'd spend the rest of my life with. My father's insistence on finishing my education before I married so I could fall back on it if I needed seemed old-fashioned and exasperating. I grudgingly finished college in three years, but his demand put me in mind of someone considering a pre-nup. Didn't he think our love would last? Dad, however, viewed this as an insurance policy.

I was wrong. He was right. I'm still as in love with my husband of thirty-two years as the day that I married him, but many women aren't as lucky in love. Those who divorce for whatever reason must survive on their own. They need a good education to find jobs that offer livable wages.

3. Save for a rainy day.

Dad graduated from high school in the Depression. He witnessed grown men selling apples to put food on the table for their families. While never stingy, he didn't believe in going into debt. His attitude was that you appreciated something more when you worked for it. From furniture to vacations, we never lived beyond our means. He stressed the proper way to use credit. Putting a lavish meal in a fancy restaurant on a credit card meant fleeting pleasure and created debt. Paying installments for a refrigerator that you would use for ten years was fine.

4. Never count on anything until you have it in your hand.

This is an offshoot of numbers one and three. It's fine to dream and live in hope, but don't gamble unless you're willing to lose. The Stock Market is like Vegas casinos— don't gamble money you can ill afford to lose. Politicians need to heed this as well. Borrowing from one program to fund another isn't solving a problem—it's just sugarcoating it.

5. There's no such thing as woman's work.

Dad, like his father before him, did everything around the house. He ran the vacuum, made delicious meals and desserts, soothed my feverish brow when needed, and generally supported my mother (who was a housewife) without making a fuss. My parents were partners in every sense of the word. He loved, protected and cared for my mother and me, allowing us freedom and independence long before the word "feminist" came into vogue.

Every day I celebrate my dad's memory. He's been gone ten years, but I see pieces of him in the man I married, in my daughter, and even in my son-in-law. He instilled values and left memories far richer than those any store can sell.

Happy Father's Day, Dad.
Your loving daughter, Michele

My Greatest Teacher

By Margaret A. Elliott

I cherish my earliest memory. I am three years old and in the tiny apartment that our family would soon vacate to move into our permanent home. My father and I sit on the edge of his bed while he teaches me how to play solitaire. He is wearing a sleeveless cotton undershirt and khaki trousers. I watch his strong, working-class hands shuffle the cards. He is young and strong and knows so much more than I.

I am sure that I did not master the game that day, but the memory is wonderful. Over our years together, he taught me many things, including his belief in a higher power. I can see him sitting at the chrome kitchen table, rosary beads in hand, from 6:45 to 7:00 each weekday evening saying his beads along with Archbishop Cushing's droning voice blaring on a Boston radio station. This nightly ritual continued throughout my childhood.

My father taught me fairness and honesty. He was a hard worker, leaving before first light each morning with his black lunch box and a thermos of coffee. He was a plumber, working for large construction companies. Much of his work was done outside in the heat of summer or in the bitter cold New England winters. I remember the thermal underwear, steel-toed work boots, sherpa-lined jackets, and hats with earflaps—gear to beat the cold, wet workdays.

Although my father was quiet and sometimes overly serious, he was congenial. Many evenings after finishing his rosary, he would take me to visit others. Sometimes we'd walk down the unpaved driveway to his sister's house. We wouldn't stay long. He'd just check in to see how her family's day had gone. Other times we'd drive to his elderly aunts' home in the next village. The aunts were gracious but frugal. The scent of home-made lye soap always filled their home. I think my father enjoyed visiting these aunts because they were his deceased mother's sisters. Through them, he felt close to her even after she had gone.

On many summer evenings, one of several apprentice plumbers would appear at our door. My father would patiently tutor these young men in math with no thought of compensation. They would sit on the front steps in the balmy evening air, working out number problems on paper. When dusk dimmed the daylight, they'd retreat to the kitchen table. After the night's studies had ended, my father would reward his students with some of my mother's home baked brownies or Toll House Cookies.

He wasn't outwardly affectionate toward my mother, but he was thoughtful. Frequently on Saturday afternoons, he and I would walk to the corner drugstore where he would order a hot fudge sundae and carry it home to surprise her.

He'd often listen to radio music. When he'd hear a favorite piece begin, he'd ask my mother to dance. Together, they seemed to float around the kitchen and parlor, humming along with the music.

A few times, when I was older, I'd pass his room at bedtime and I'd spy him kneeling beside his bed, praying. I'd then crawl into my own bed, content and safe, knowing that this good man was right with the world and his Maker.

He taught me more than any credentialed teacher ever did about faith, caring, and service. He taught me well.

What's In a Name?

By Vanessa Moore

My father, the late Kenneth Moore, compassionate parent and firm disciplinarian, imparted innumerable life lessons. Among them was the importance of respecting people by addressing them by their proper names.

I grew up during the late sixties and early seventies, an era marked by civil unrest and social upheaval throughout America's urban areas. During those turbulent years, it was popular, if not fashionable, to refer to police officers as "pigs."

I still remember that warm summer night. A bunch of us kids were hanging out on the front steps of my Washington, D.C. childhood home. As many of the houses on the block where I lived weren't air conditioned, we young people often remained outdoors until around 11:00 p.m. when temperatures cooled down. There we were, about six of us, sitting on the steps that adjoined the front porch. I was around twelve years old.

Along came two police officers strolling down the street across from us. When they had walked about a half-block past us, we all shouted, "pig, pig!" We even threw in a few "oinks" for emphasis. During that time, the police were fairly tolerant of such verbal insults, degrading though they were. The two officers merely ignored us and kept walking their beat.

Unbeknownst to me, my father was standing just inside the storm door behind us and overheard the vile taunts. He opened the door, kindly dispersed my friends to their homes, and called my brother and me inside. Once indoors, my father calmly but sternly lectured us about the disrespectfulness of "calling people outside of their names."

Sure, we tried to convince him that it wasn't so bad, that everybody called police officers "pigs." What harm was there in uttering an innocent three-letter word? What about freedom of speech? I mean, it's not like we threw rocks or bottles at the officers. My father listened but he wasn't moved. I imagine having grown up in the South during the forties and fifties, when African-Americans were often referred to in derogatory terms, my father probably learned a few life lessons about the harmfulness of name-calling. Anyway, he was unequivocal on the matter. We were not to refer to police officers as "pigs," and that was that. We were also forbidden to refer to any person outside of his or her proper name.

This invaluable lesson has had a lasting impact on my life. Needless to say, I never again referred to police officers as "pigs." Furthermore, I will not call an obese person "fatty," and I won't refer to someone with low intelligence as "stupid," or someone exhibiting deranged behavior as "crazy." To this day, I am so respectful of peoples' names that whenever I'm unsure about the correct enunciation, I'll preface my rendition by first saying to them: *"Please correct me if I'm not pronouncing your name right."*

From this one incident, I learned a great deal about respect. So what's in a name you ask? My father taught me that lesson abundantly well. His answer? *Everything.*

Lessons from a Committed Father

By Barbara S. Greenstreet

A wise minister once told me that the secret to a successful marriage is not financial security, good health, nor even love. The secret to a truly successful, lasting marriage—and emotionally healthy family life—is *commitment*.

Commitment was a key part of my father's character. He didn't lecture us about honoring commitments; it was simply the way he lived. It has taken me years of reflection in unexpected moments to appreciate how much he taught.

A pro at changing diapers, my father was an "involved" dad before it was trendy. As a young mother, I once bemoaned the late hours spent walking my first baby to sleep. "YOU, of all the kids to complain!" exclaimed Dad, who had spent many a night walking the floor with me on his shoulder. It was Dad who gave the small children baths in our family, and it was in those bath times, three kids to a tub, that he taught us his favorite songs. In his gravelly, slightly off-key voice he sang his beloved country music. We could all sing "Wabash Cannonball" along with Roy Acuff, and Hank Williams' mournful ballads were as familiar to us as nursery rhymes.

Dad kept a loving, steadfast bond to one wife for 37 years, held one job for 41 years. His commitment to our church was strong; over more than three decades he headed virtually every board or committee. Our minister remembered, "If there was an usher needed, or volunteer requested, Austin would step forward. If there was a clean-up day, or a potluck supper—Austin would be there; in fact, he would probably be leading it." Commitment to church meant more than just showing up in a pew on Sunday morning, and fatherhood meant more than just bringing home a paycheck.

Committed fatherhood also went beyond singing with the kids. Dad and Mom raised five teenagers during the turbulent '60's and '70's. They honored their commitment as parents even when the phone rang with messages they didn't want to hear:

> "Hello, Mom and Dad? I, uh, had a problem at school. I'm in detention. Will you pick me up?"
>
> "Hi, Dad. I'm moving out of the dorm to rent a house with my boyfriend. No, he doesn't go to college, he's a rock singer."
>
> "Hello, Mr. Sheldon? This is the police department. I'm sorry to wake you. There's been a car accident. Your daughters will be OK, but your car is not drivable."

My father suffered much in those years, I'm sure. But never was it suggested that anything we did could ever cut us off from him. I'm glad that this was so, for by honoring that pledge to parenthood in spite of the difficult times, Dad remained available to us for the happier phone calls, too:

> "Dad, I passed my exams! You'll be here for graduation, won't you?"
>
> "Dad, we want to be married in September. Yes, the traditional way… You get to walk me down the aisle!"
>
> "Hey, Dad—you're going to be a grandfather!"

The phone lines were also open for the heart-wrenching calls he himself made to each one of us kids:

> "Hello, Bub? (*my childhood nickname*) Your mother and I just got back from the doctors. The test results aren't good. The cancer has spread to my liver, and other organs too. Looks like there's nothing more they can do. The bottom line is, well, it'll all be over in six months………. Bub? Are you there? I love you."

For all his steadfastness, lived out in every day life, my father was a quiet, reserved, even shy man. The phrase "I love you" was not bandied about easily in our family. I'm glad that in his final weeks Dad was able to say it more freely.

In those final days, I sat tongue-tied in grief and shock as Dad declined far more quickly than the doctors had predicted. I wanted to tell him what a great dad he had been. I wanted to let him know I remembered him playing "whale" and "tidal wave" in the backyard wading pool with us on hot summer days. I wanted to say how much I loved his corny, pun-laden sense of humor (in spite of all the groans whenever he made one of his jokes).

I wanted to hear about what was important in his life. I thought there was much he had done and seen that I didn't know. But his words to me in that hospital room were not of his travels in The War, or of his career. His words, as he reviewed his life, were, "I've been pretty lucky. I have the greatest kids."

Twelve years later, I still miss Dad—I guess the missing never goes away. But, I too have been lucky. I had the greatest father, who taught me in deed and action about unconditional love and commitment.

"One touch of nature makes the whole world kin."

– William Shakespeare

The Fishing

By Gail Kavanagh

There was a tree—I think it was called the Hawthorn—that grew profusely in Ireland when I was a child. We called it the bread and butter tree, because you could eat the leaves. Nature never let you go hungry.

My father was a simple man, not given to long speeches or putting the world to rights by laying down rules and regulations of behavior. He believed in nature, and a God who made the world for man and animals to share.

He believed, too, in nurturing whatever talent you were given, so when I showed an aptitude for writing, he took great pleasure and pride in that.

One Christmas I discovered a marvelous present from him; a small plastic typewriter, complete with a stack of paper and two new ribbons. It was a toy, but it really worked, even if the printed letters were uneven.

I knew exactly what I was going to do with this wonderful present. I was going to write a great story, as good as one of those books my mother read all the time, when the potatoes were burning and the fire was going out, and people would say, "Oh, there's Maire, with her nose stuck in a book again."

I would make a great show of clearing a space for it on the tiny table I used for a desk, stack up the sheets of paper beside it, and sit down seriously to write my great novel. My father, who was always busy in the evenings with some craft project of his own, would look at me over the top of his glasses and say, "Now, what are you going to write about?" And I could never think of anything to write about.

One night he tapped his pipe on the table, and said, "Why don't you write about the fishing?"

He had woken me up that morning at 3 a.m. The dawn of that day was a sulky, dark, grudging thing, creeping out from behind the hills and shrugging into a worn overcoat. I was right in tune with it as I stumbled out of bed. I hadn't felt like going fishing. My father carried his rod, a creel for the fish and little else. He might not even use the rod, being adept at "tickling" a fat trout into the creel.

We started out, following the river upstream and pausing at various places for Dad to cast his line and wait patiently, pipe steaming, for a bite. I sat myself beside him on the bank. It was almost summer, but no one had told the weather that. The grey mist was slowly giving way, but the clouds still billowed above, promising rain later in the day.

The river danced past over a rocky bed. Dad had dropped the line in a deep hole, but the rod refused to twitch.

"Do you see the rabbit?" Dad said suddenly.

"What rabbit?" I put my head up like a retriever; as if I expected him to tell me go fetch it. Indeed, with that quizzical sense of humor, he might have.

He pointed with his pipe across to the opposite bank. I strained my eyes among the reeds but could see nothing.

"Further up, near those trees," he said. "There are two stalks of grass that aren't stalks of grass at all."

I looked harder, and then I saw a twitch, and a swift movement, but the rabbit was gone before I could get a good look at it.

"There now," he commented, "you sit surrounded by all this life and industry and you see none of it." He laughed. "Do you know why the rabbit took off?"

"No, was it afraid of us?"

"It was afraid of the fox. Sniff the wind coming over here. Can you smell it?"

I sniffed, and caught the traces of a rank odor.

"Let's go further upstream," he said. "There's no fish here."

He reeled in the line, and we walked on to where the river bubbled into a small weir. There was a likely looking fishing hole here, deep and mysterious. As we crossed to the other bank through the shallows to reach the fishing hole, I noticed eddies of small silver fish in the shallow pools.

"Do you have your net with you? We might have a breakfast of sprats when we get home."

I had my net crammed into one pocket of my jacket and a jam jar in the other, with string tied around the neck for carrying. Not much of a fisherman myself, I could scoop up sprats with the best of them. They were delicious fried in butter and served on toasted bread. I filled my jar while Dad found himself a spot on the bank, and cast his line into the fishing hole. There was slapping sound from the water and I knew there were trout here, so I crept up onto the bank, stowing my jam jar between two stones, and lay down to watch my dad's fishing line snake through the air.

The heavy clouds began to thin out, with small patches of blue. Maybe it would not rain after all. I could hear a dog barking in the distance as the Angelus bells started to ring, calling the population to worship.

We did not go to church, but my father laid down his rod and gazed quietly at the beauty around him, and I did the same, and felt my soul fill with a joy that is almost impossible to describe. The wind shifted the trees, and the tolling of the bells struck deep in my heart. This was our simple worship, and when my father was done offering his soul in thanks for the fine trout lying on the bank, and the beauty of the morning, we got up softly and began the long trek back to the wagon. Somewhere a tractor roared into life, signaling the start of a working day for the settled people.

We walked in companiable silence, my dad with his reel and his trout, and me with my brimming jam jar.

Dad woke my mother by waving the fresh trout under her nose. I started to work getting a fire ready to fry the sprats. Dad cooked them himself, stirring them in the butter until they were fragrant and golden, while I made the toast, hooking thick slicing of bread on a bent coat hanger and dangling them in front of the flames.

But later that night, when he told me to write about the fishing, all I wrote was, "I went fishing with Dad this morning. He caught two trout."

He often told me to listen, and look, and learn from the world around me, and find God in the gentle movement of the breeze, the waves on the sea, or the quick dart of a hare.

After he died, in 1981, I knew he had left me something of incalculable value, for my faith has never left me, and is refreshed by the simple ritual of getting back in touch with the natural world he loved so well. It is this very simple faith that I believe has served as a bedrock for my life, and, I hope, for my children's lives.

And now I have written about the fishing.

Family Trees

By Linda J. Parker

In North America every year on an undetermined day, sometime between March and May, it happens again. Each time, our winter-weary hearts are mildly surprised and genuinely awed by the occurrence—spring makes a dramatic return.

Life announces annual renewal, confirmed with an extravagant display of color. While the botanical names vary across the countryside, the presentation is always spectacular. Paint buckets of color in shades of cherry blossom, dogwood, daffodil, azalea, and tulip are lavishly splashed across the landscape.

Even those who lack poetry in their souls are touched by the beauty of a pathway lined in pink blossoms or a hillside aflutter with creamy white petals. Cities celebrate festivals to honor foliage in bloom. Newspapers cast aside their detailing of disasters to showcase color photography of the seasonal brilliance. Everyone is overwhelmed all over again by spring flowers that we are certain are the most beautiful they have ever been.

Everyone, except my dad. Oh, he admires the impressive dogwood and redbud trees that grow in our hometown, and he never fails to appreciatively acknowledge the budding heads of crocus and Easter lilies. However, spring's showier displays do not distract him. He is simply amazed by *green*. While others delight in technicolor trees, my father studies spring hillsides, enthralled by the number of shades of *green*.

For eighteen years, my dad and I shared spring together. I watched the strongest, smartest, center-of-my-universe man, set aside his daily tasks to marvel at *green*.

"Look," he would say, "at how many variations spring creates in the color *green.*" Nothing else would need to be said.

For a few weeks, each tree would seem hand-painted in its own custom-blended color. By midsummer, these same trees would all turn to a single, uniform shade of summertime *green.*

For the nearly thirty years since I left home, my dad and I have had to make do with the sharing of spring by long distance. Each year, he brings up the topic of *green*. Each year, we are amazed all over again.

The strongest, smartest, center-of-my-universe man has traded some of his strengths for others. Time grants greater insight while it is busy stealing the sharp-eyed vision of youth. Wisdom grows stronger as muscle mass declines. Perspective broadens and becomes more flexible, all the while bones grow brittle and joints become stiff.

In recent years, I have prayed in hospitals and by my father's bedside; humble prayers for his healing and well being. I have prayed selfishly because I want so much to keep him—even long distance—in my life.

Years are slipping past us and I know that one day the answer to my prayers will not be the answer I want to hear. However, I also know that I will never truly be without my dad. When the hand of my heavenly Father renews the earth each spring, I will again share the season long distance with my dad. I will marvel at hillsides and their amazing diversity of greens. It will make me feel, as it always does, inconsequential yet astoundingly special and blessed. And I am certain that when God chooses to bring my dad home to Him, He will forever mark spring with an even greater display of the variations of green. James Parker passed away March 12, 2004.

Of Men and Mountains

By Kristine Lowder

Old timers called it "Mountain Fever." My first exposure was in 1964. I was four years old and "infected" for life, thanks mostly to my dad, Tom Naas.

He called it "The Mountain." Just like the locals. In the Great Northwest no one ever asks, "Which one?" We don't have to. Folks who've lived in the Evergreen State all their lives still stop and stare when The Mountain reveals himself. He's that impressive.

Rising like a monumental moon above the menagerie of motels, cabins, lodges, and bunk houses that freckle his feet, the King of the Cascades dwarfs the Space Needle, the crowded tarmac of SeaTac Airport, and the spidery steel of Seattle's Safeco Field. Indeed, The Mountain rises above everything that lives and everything that doesn't in Washington, as far as the eye can see.

When "The Mountain is out," as we locals say, Mount Rainier can be seen from Canada to Oregon, from the San Juan Islands to Spokane. When hidden behind his own weather, The Mountain can still be seen on personal checks, bowling lanes, postcards, beer labels, billboard ads, and the license plate of every vehicle registered in the Evergreen State. But for me, The Mountain began with my dad.

It was time to leave. My parents swept the floor, emptied the trash, closed and locked the front door of the Ohanapecosh staff apartment at Mount Rainier National Park. An educator, Tom Naas spent his summers as a park ranger for the National Park Service in the early '60s. My family spent those summers at Grand Teton National Park in Wyoming and later at Mount Rainier. It was 1966, just after Labor Day. Dad's seasonal rangering duties at Mount Rainier wound down and so did our summer stay at Ohana staff housing. It was time to head home, back to Southern California for another school year.

Groaning under a gargantuan luggage rack, Dad's blue Chevy churned out the miles on our three-day return trip to San Diego. Restless for our return to The Mountain, I eagerly anticipated the following summer even before we crossed the threshold of our San Diego front door. Little did I guess that my return to The Mountain would take nearly four decades.

The seventh of eight children, Tom Naas was born in Detroit, Michigan in 1925. Tall and angular, he carried himself with the easy gait of an athlete. He lettered in basketball, football, and track, made the All-State basketball team, and played semi-pro hockey. On the playing field or in the classroom, when Tom looked at people, spoke to them, his eyes often laughed and sparkled as though he knew something they didn't. Boyishly handsome with an outrageous shock of dark hair, his blue eyes were clear, direct and quiet.

Tom served with the Army Air Forces in Italy during WWII and then earned degrees in Education from Michigan State Normal College and Eastern Michigan University. He married Margaret "Peggy" LaFleur in 1951 and taught school in Detroit. Tom and Peg moved to California in the '50's to pursue their teaching careers. Together they raised me, my two brothers, and my kid sister.

I grew up confusing Dad and John Wayne. To me they were both "larger than life." Tom was a "strong, silent type." Like The Duke, Dad never said much but when he did, we kids listened up. And right quick. Like the Saturday night I asked Dad for permission to skip the morrow's Sunday school and church service. I'd been invited to go horse backing. Bounding over hill and dale aboard a sleek Quarter horse promised a lot more excitement than Mrs. Jerman's next lesson on blind Bartameaus. I was in the fourth grade. Horses were next to God. Maybe better.

Dad's response was typical and unequivocal: "No." The steel edge in his voice told me the subject was closed. That and *The Look*. Medusa had nothing on Dad and *The Look*.

Dad was offered a permanent Park Service position in 1966 after rangering three summers at Mount Rainier. He turned the Park Service down in favor of his professional passion: Education. He taught at the elementary and secondary levels for many years and was later a guidance counselor.

Not surprisingly, Dad never said much about the guidance he found in his Christian faith, not even when Mom passed away at the age of 54.

Dad remarried four years later. He continued living his faith, a quiet obedience over seven decades. He opened his home for Bible studies, served on building and finance committees, and sang tenor in the church choir. It wasn't until after I lost him to cancer at age 77 that I began to appreciate the depth of his devotion to God and his love for his Savior.

Before that, the greatest conundrum of my dad's life was probably his detached, taciturn personality. The "strong, silent type" wore thin after awhile.

"How come we never get past sports and the weather?" I groused to my husband, Chris, after a weekend visit to San Diego. "How come *I* always have to initiate a conversation? His hands aren't broken. Why can't *Dad* pick up the phone?"

I'm told that Dad exuded warmth and graciousness to others like a sunflower opening to the summer sun, but I rarely saw it. Maybe I was looking in the wrong direction. I realize now that what I interpreted as "aloof detachment" was more a product of Dad's upbringing and generation than a lack of caring. Maybe we were both looking in the wrong direction.

"He didn't want to pry into your personal lives," my step mom, Barbara, explained shortly after I arrived in San Diego for the July memorial service. "Your dad always said, 'If my kids want me to know anything, they'll tell me.' That was his attitude." When she suggested he take the initiative to keep in touch, call "just to talk" or that "the kids" didn't know he felt that way, Dad's response was, "You mean I've been doing it wrong all these years?"

"All these years" tumbled into decades and it was June 2003 before I knew it. My sister flew in from San Diego to join us for a camping trip to Mount Rainier and a hiking jaunt to Paradise, just north of the park headquarters in Longmire.

Roosting like an alpine aerie amid the sweet, thin air and pristine snow of Paradise, the circular construction of Henry M. Jackson Visitor's Center resembles a Star Wars space station stuck in the Ice Age. Inside, Laura and I prowled the gift shop for something for Dad.

"I bet Dad would like this," I mused, thumbing through a copy of Floyd Schmoe's *A Year in Paradise*. I had recently finished reading the memoirs of the park's first naturalist. Dad would enjoy it. He never commented on the cacophony of color swashing the world-famous Paradise flower fields each summer. But I remembered piling out of the Chevy for a family hike or a picnic and looking at Dad as he took in the Renoir pastels of a sea of alpine blossoms. Hands on hips, tanned arms reaching down to hoist me aboard his shoulders, Dad's smile could've lit up the entire park.

We bought the Schmoe book. Laura carted it back to San Diego and gave it to Dad. The cancer had him confined to bed most of the time. Reading was one of his remaining pleasures. A voracious reader who devoured books like Shamu gobbling sardines, Dad finished all 300 pages of the Paradise book in one day. I liked the fact that we could connect through something I learned to cherish from him: a good book. Three weeks later Dad entered another Paradise.

When my stepmom emailed me from San Diego in mid-July, she suggested I catch a plane soon. "Your dad's taken a turn for the worse," she wrote. "It appears that he has little time left. How soon can you come?" I snagged the next doable flight south. And just missed him. My plane touched down at Lindbergh Field on July 21, two days after Dad's Coronation Day.

Two months later I returned to Mount Rainier National Park for a family camping trip. Chris and our boys pitched the tent in the *A Loop* of the Ohana campground, just down the hill from the ranger station my dad once manned. We hiked one of Dad's favorite trails to roaring Silver Falls. The years fell away as we chugged over the rich red earth hemming the Ohana Visitor's Center and Laughingwater Creek.

I took the dog out early the next morning. Eve and I marched over the campground roads I once "helped" patrol with my dad, perched atop his Park Service motor scooter. Sandwiched between his bear paw hands, I nestled against the scratchy stiffness of his gray and green Park Service uniform, his omnipresent "Smokey the Bear" Stetson tipped back to accommodate my head.

The western loops of the Ohanapecosh campground were closed after the busy hustle and bustle of the summer season. Eve pulled on her blue leash, yanking me down to a creek that cuts through the campground's *D Loop*. I waded in that creek as a five year-old.

While Chris lit the Coleman camp stove and herded our four boys into breakfast duties, I steered our faithful Yellow Labrador toward a pine-needled path just over the bridge spanning the aqua waters of the churning Ohanapecosh River. A series of four inch drainage holes crease the shoulders of that bridge at eight foot intervals. I couldn't resist. I tossed a pebble into each one, watching as the Ohana's icy blue waters swallowed it whole. The pebble tossing was a summer bridge ritual I'd adopted as a four year-old. Four decades later, it was automatic.

I knew the trail to the Ohanapecosh Amphitheater. I'd walked it dozens of times as a kid. Eve and I ambled into the open air amphitheater where Dad delivered weekend lectures on everything from forest flora and fauna to park history to proper food storage. I was glad to be alone, just Eve and me.

The amphitheater seemed smaller than I remember, but the cement fire ring is still there, off to the right side. Ditto the gently sloping platform, screen, and the omnipresent Park Service "arrow" emblem.

The morning was quiet as I meandered toward the back row of pine benches and sat down. Ohana's anemic morning sunshine struggled for supremacy with the park's omnipresent dew. Drenched with overnight rain, soaring hemlocks and western red cedar dripped with liquid diamonds. Gray-headed camp robbers argued over snack stashes. Squirrels and chipmunks perched on chubby haunches, pausing warily in their never-ending search for food.

I sat on a back bench, shoulders quaking. "Dad!" Eve didn't protest as I threw my arms around her neck and buried my face in her sleek blond fur. The grief was sharp and sudden, yet I couldn't help feeling, even in my loss, an assurance I couldn't define.

Sobbing, I realized the goodness of a loving God whose timing is neither too early nor too late. I slowly understood that my return to The Mountain unfolded in His way, in His time. In the 36 years I had been away, He chose to bring me back when He knew I needed it most: just after one of The Mountain's choicest rangers departed for good.

It seems an unwritten yet tragic rule of life that we often don't see things clearly until they're out of the picture. Permanently. A wistful sadness, a melancholy loss accompanies the obvious.

Nearly 40 years since the last time I gawked at glorious Mount Rainier with my dad, The King of the Cascades stands as bold and impressive as ever. A supreme monarch ruling his domain, The Mountain stands gold and glittering in the evening sun, perhaps the most "permanent" and venerated private icon of the Great Northwest.

Permanence is a pleasant delusion.

Returning home later, I scanned the contents of a faded photo album. The brittle pages creaked in protest as I flipped them until I found it: a 1964 photo of a skinny snow-suited six year-old. Me. In that photo my older brother and I stand on a snow field just above Paradise in Mount Rainier National Park. Next to the creased black and white snapshot I mounted a photo of me and my family, posed on the same Paradise snow field in 2003.

I've changed since 1964. I'm not alone. Dad is gone. The Mountain remains, but it too is changing. Deteriorating. Glaciers gnaw at its shoulders; avalanches carve its vales and meadows. It too will eventually crumble into dust. Together, memories and Mountain stand shrouded in the treble mists of time, mystery, and truth.

One of the truths stretching between that '64 snapshot and the richer, more robust photo of 2003 is four decades of selfless guidance from a faithful father. I realize now that I never really knew him. I understood even less. However, I see that he gifted me with treasures beyond tangibility: education, learning, perseverance, quiet courage. And more.

Some things Dad taught because they were a natural outgrowth of who he was, like respect for God's creation. Or the importance of passing on a family legacy to the next generation. That's one reason I write and read. Dad read aloud to me early and often. My earliest memories involve snuggling into Dad's lap with a book as he narrated the adventures of Peter Pan and Wendy, Billy and Blaze, Charlie and the Chocolate Factory, or Curious George.

It's not surprising that my love for the printed page, instilled primarily by my dad, eventually brought forth its own fruit. After that first "A" in my seventh grade Creative Writing class, Dad encouraged me to develop my journalistic skills and practice, practice, practice. He was my first and best writing coach. He taught. I improved and learned. About family, faith, and the brevity of life. About men and mountains. And that the two may have more in common than we may think.

Both can evidence solidity, sturdiness, silence. Clipped sentences, birthday cards, occasional phone calls. Avalanches, mud slides, boulders tossed from shifting glaciers. Neither may say much. But when they do, we best listen. They're saying something worth hearing. Quietly faithful, regularly reliable, mountains and men can be so predictable and routine that we take them for granted. How easily we forget about the eroding mountain, the cancer leeching life from a loved one.

Permanence is a pleasant delusion, in both man and mountain.

Not long after Dad's death I spotted Mount Rainier on a clear day. The King of the Cascades donned ermine mantle, stretched to his 14,410-foot glory, and towered over the Washington landscape like a snowy colossus. I stood rooted a moment, gazing at The Mountain. The dual daggers of

Reminiscence and Regret plunged deep as I teetered between a smile and tears. And then I chose.

It's not "The Mountain" anymore. For me, the Cascade King is a Monument. A memorial carved once again from the treble mists of time, truth and memories. So when I see Rainier now, I smile as a salute to my dad: Tom Naas, Mountain of a Man.

Inconsistencies

By Deborah Straw

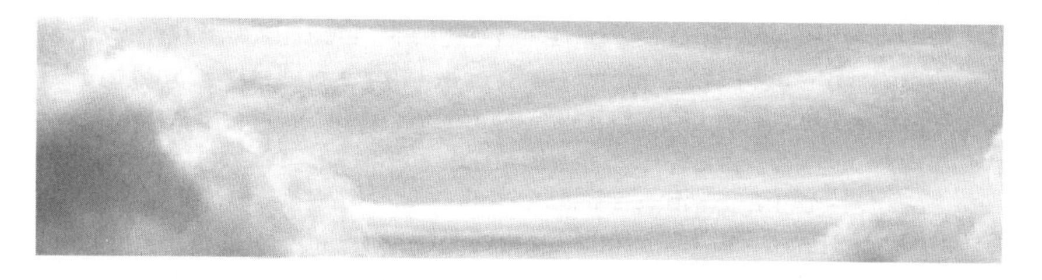

Albert Schweitzer is one of my heroes.

So is my dad.

That presents a bit of a problem. You see, Dr. Schweitzer coined a philosophy he called "reverence for life." He considered all creatures worthy and never wanted to kill even a mosquito. A doctor, musician, theologian, and vegetarian, he spent more than half his life treating lepers and others in Africa. As I read more and more books by and about him, he helped me become more respectful of and grateful for all creatures. I now am loath to kill a mosquito, too.

My dad, Donald Straw, who died six years ago of emphysema, was a consummate fisherman. Before that, he had been a hunter of deer, squirrels, and other wild creatures. But, in middle age, he gave that up because he loved and revered nature. He grew up in an agricultural society, however, where fishing and hunting were what men did. Nobody questioned this.

Born in 1908, one of fourteen children, Dad was raised on a Vermont farm. His parents had dairy cows, a pair of gigantic draft horses, and barn cats. If a cat had kittens, Dad often had the task of drowning them in the brook. It didn't bother his conscience when he was a young boy. But as he aged, traveled quite extensively in the U.S. and Canada, moved around, and married my mother, his attitudes about the value and beauty of other species changed radically. Except for the fish.

An only child who enjoyed spending time alone with each of my parents, I went fishing with my dad. My parents were not at all athletic; they were disinterested in team sports and would never have joined a gym. My mom tells me that Dad was athletic early on, but when I knew him he was most certainly not. My mom can't ride a bicycle; my dad couldn't swim. But they did love to camp, fish from the shore or from a small rowboat, and cook over an open fire. Often while Mom cooked potatoes and chicken over the campfire, Dad and I headed down to the stream.

One of the earliest photos I have is a scallop-edged black and white Kodak of me with pigtails, at about age five, holding a gigantic brown trout. I am smiling; my dad took the shot. Although in some ways he would have preferred me to be a boy, to share his male enthusiasms, I did enjoy fishing, a sport I continued into my late teens.

A decade later, my husband took over my pole and place on the bank with Dad, and I stuck to my nature worship and writing career. I discovered Albert Schweitzer and his animal philosophy; I began to collect his books. The notion of fishing became somewhat anathema to me, but I never mentioned it to Dad or Mom.

The greatest gift I got from my father, aside from, perhaps, sensitivity for the underdog and a love of reading, was not a passion for fishing (which I never developed) but a love of nature. As an older man, Dad was engrossed in nature. It was his first priority: to learn about other creatures, to study them, to talk about and write about them. He read books on dogs, cats, birds, and butterflies, and he wrote stories about Foxy, their long-haired cat, or "the fish that got away." Unlike me, he never developed a love of city life. Where would he have been able to find wildflowers for Mom or hang his hummingbird feeder in a primarily concrete landscape?

Dad was able to feed birdseeds to sparrows and chickadees from his hand, and, with Mom, pampered one cat after another. When Foxy died, it almost broke his heart. He sometimes rescued orphaned squirrels or chipmunks, nurturing them on our screened porch, releasing them when they were stronger.

One of his and Mom's favorite activities was taking rides on dirt roads going nowhere. The highlight of these trips was seeing a woodpecker, or a herd of Holsteins, or a few wild turkeys, or a patch of wildflowers. Mom recently told me Dad would wade into a swamp to pick wildflowers, like marsh marigolds, that she admired. "Not all men would do that, you know," she said. I know.

But he never gave up fishing, not until he had to. When he developed emphysema and was attached to a bulky oxygen tank all day and night, he stopped going outside so much. Was it embarrassment or the hassle of lugging the tank around? He was weaker; he had lost height and a lot of weight. At any rate, he no longer drove or went fishing. During this time, I wrote a poem to him called "The First Fishless Summer." It was nearly as painful for me to see him give up his sixty-year avocation as it was for him to stop. The first and second year that he didn't go out, on the first day of fishing season, I couldn't look at the streambeds because I would feel sad Dad wasn't there. In fact, in the six years since he has been gone, I still fantasize that the slim, older man I see casting over the stream is him, in another time and another place.

I believe Dad's attachment to fishing was mostly about being outdoors, alone, in the quiet, fresh air. That kept him fishing, but perhaps there was also something atavistic about it—the last segments of being some sort of a hunter/gatherer to fulfill his masculine image of himself. He enjoyed the entire ritual: getting up very early, taking along a packed lunch, digging or buying a few worms, and walking through dew-drenched fields to the banks of a river, most likely the Mad River in Waitsfield and Warren, Vermont. This was the area where he was born; he loved this river more than any other. He taught my husband, Bruce, to fish there; the two enjoyed their pensive times standing on the shores, waiting. It was necessary to be extremely quiet, something both men liked, especially as both lived with talkative women. It hardly mattered to Bruce if he caught anything—he is allergic to fish, anyway—but he went faithfully for the joy of spending special time with my father. Finally, my dad had the son he had always wanted to fish with. Bruce even learned to dress fish—with gloves on so his allergies didn't flare up. Mom and I gladly ate their fresh brookies and rainbows.

I stopped fishing when I could no longer stand taking the bloody hook out of the trout's mouth, or looking in its cold, still eye. I could still eat them, but I wanted no part in their actual demise. (A recent study conducted by the Royal Society in Great Britain has reinforced my feelings: they found that "rainbow trout are shown to feel pain," pain akin to what mammals feel.) I am still not a vegetarian, but if I had to kill my meat, I would be.

My dad's (and my mom's) love of wild places has remained with me. I'd rather live outside in a big, secure tent, to be close to nature, than be what I consider trapped inside a huge, perfect, air-conditioned house. Spring means gardening and the intensity of birdcalls to me, not spring cleaning or buying a new wardrobe. I may not fish, but I still love watching Holsteins, taking rides on dirt roads with no destination, and having picnics near streams. I will pick wildflowers on any dry piece of land but don't trust swamps as Dad did. I photograph animals, birds, and flowers whenever I can.

Life is full of inconsistencies. The fact that my dad loved fishing and revered all of nature is a bit confusing, but I doubt he was troubled by this inconsistency. The fact that I spend most of my waking hours caring for and writing about non-human creatures—and about their ethical treatment—yet I still eat meat and wear leather shoes is somewhat inconsistent. We all have our limits, our priorities, our blind spots.

I always knew Dad's fishing was not to be questioned. Fishing helped define him. He was a man of the woods and the fields who enjoyed waking early, walking through cornfields, listening to bird songs, and standing on the banks of Vermont's streams, feeling free and at peace.

"Courage is resistance to fear, mastery of fear - not absence of fear."

– Mark Twain

Last Flight

By Dara Armstrong Lehner

He was a tough old bird, my father, definitely from a different era. From my earliest remembrances, Daddy was always in an Air Force flight suit, very tall, and always disciplined. In his day, a flight instructor either had to have nerves of steel or none at all to do the job. This came in handy years later when he taught his five children how to drive.

Dad had his own strict philosophy and methods of teaching battle flight survival. He would pepper his stories of aerial dogfights with a healthy dose of reality to capture our young imaginations and hold them in rapt attention for days. He touched a spirit deep within me that has always longed to fly as he had, yet that is a dream unfulfilled. His sense of freedom and adventure was aptly conveyed to me and flourishes to this day. However, in the restricted era of my youth, women were to be protected and discouraged from pursuing such adventurous deeds, including by my own demonstrative father.

My father's passion for teaching translated into his love and knowledge of many styles of music and photography as well. He could pick up and play any musical instrument by ear. We children all have a wide range of musical interests, thanks to him. Three of his children play band and orchestral instruments yet today. One of them has become a celebrated high school band director, and I have inherited his teaching legacy and obvious passion for life and photography.

Part of my father's legacy as the consummate teacher was to instill in his children mental toughness and a willingness to take a vocal stand to fight for our beliefs. He survived arduous battles both in the military and later in business. His toughest battle, however, was his last battle with lung cancer, which ravaged his body to a shell.

After a bleak prognosis of only a month to live, Daddy fought for nine months; that was the fighter pilot in him. He kept surprising us all as he routinely set goals for survival. Daddy demonstrated daily his mental strength and courage to wage war on his silent enemy who had so tenaciously taken a stronghold over his body.

This time, there were no special weapons attached to his beloved plane, to soar and blast the invasive cells from his deteriorating body. His mental toughness demonstrated to all who knew him his tenacious and stubborn nature to conquer whatever obstacles arose.

It was one final lesson for us—to be strong in the face of adversity, to stand up and do battle with any enemy trying to cut us off from those whom we love, and how to die with dignity, even as it threatens to be robbed from you. He continued to look at life as an adventurous journey. Dad knew his battle was coming to a close, yet he was presenting to all of us a special gift crafted over a lifetime.

Then one dreary, rainy day in June, seven years ago, Daddy took his last glorious flight. After his somber memorial service, we all gathered, umbrella clad family and friends, at the cemetery to pay homage to one tough old bird, this man of wings. A flag-draped coffin, a rhythmic twenty-one-gun salute, and a soulful rendition of "Taps" by a lone stoic trumpeter caused tears of grief, relief, and even joy to flow, all our pent up emotions released. This was our final send off with respect and honor for a husband, father, friend, and pilot on his last flight.

Fly high, Daddy!

My Own Unexpected Party

By Julie Atkin

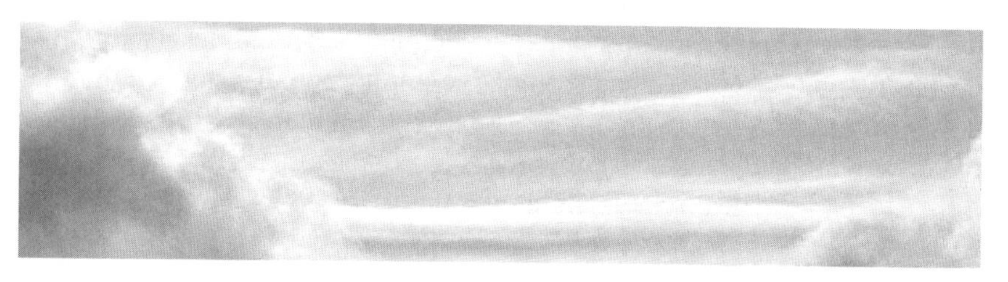

The excitement and adventure that started in Chapter 1 of J.R.R. Tolkien's *The Hobbit*, appropriately titled "The Unexpected Party," both worried me and yet thrilled me. It's not that I ever really expected a powerful and wise wizard draped in white robes to show up at my doorstep and call me out on an adventure of danger, fortune and great deeds. Yet I still worried about the potential dangers and consequences of something like that happening to me. If Bilbo Baggins had the quintessential hobbit life (with friends and a warm and cozy home filled with books to read), why on earth would he abandon his home to endure the dangers of giant spiders and a slimy cave-creature with dual personalities? All for some speculative ring?

I asked my father this question one night twenty years ago. It was a school night, and he was making dinner for my two sisters, mom, and me. Without turning around, he asked, "Why are you going to go off to college in a few years?"

At the time, I found his reply both amusing and misunderstood. I was fifteen, so most of the time I found a lot of what my parents said off point and ridiculous. College was simply something expected of me. It was just another step in my education, and I had been told that everyone who wanted a good job went to college. I really never examined my role in this situation; I just knew that I was going to go. Although I was unsure why he chose that question as an answer to my "hobbit dilemma," something stuck with me. He had answered my question with a question, which ultimately helped me figure out the answer myself.

My father could have given me blanket answer, like, "He left for an adventure," or, "Adventure is good." And I would have believed him all the same. As kids we are told that a lot of things are good: obeying your parents, eating vegetables, staying in school. And we accept it as an abstract, not always seeing ourselves in the equation. But my father's question made me think, and it put me in this equation, and in the adventure.

In my own life, I have had many adventures and have stepped into the new and the unknown many times. College, love, marriage, mistakes that have hurt me and others, triumphs over obstacles, parenthood, art, and even my father's death, have all shown up at my doorstep in place of an aged wizard.

I came to understand what he was trying to teach me twenty years ago, and I am still learning. I learn it everyday. Why do we move forward and embark on life's adventures, sometimes with choice and sometimes without? Because we can. And we learn in those adventures who we really are as we see ourselves from another point of view. It makes us better. In that gray area between black and white, where it is uncertain and has not yet become, we learn. We learn that we CAN be brave, we CAN be leaders, we CAN make mistakes, we CAN forgive, we CAN laugh and have a really, really good time, we CAN be a part of something bigger than ourselves—in both life and death even if we don't entirely understand it, we CAN love.

My father's question helped me see the process of how I can learn about myself and others in the world through my own adventures. I saw in that question why I go out in the unknown and how I learn. It made me revel in the hobbit's adventure and I felt brave enough to join him. If my college plans were considered an adventure and not just a step in life, then I was an adventurer too! Aided with this knowledge, I challenged myself and relished the journey. I started to embrace this when I set out for college several years ago, and I am still learning it as I embrace motherhood and my love affair with story telling in film and theater. I understand why Bilbo left his home for his adventure. I know my father did too, and I am grateful to have been a part of his adventure.

Dinah Might

By Tom Basinski

In 1970 at the age of 14, I found a cigar box buried in my father's workshop in the basement. It contained a group of service medals that I had never seen before. When my father got home from work that night, I produced the cigar box and asked him what the medals meant. He replied, "They are nothing special, everyone got them." Still curious, I asked my dad, "Are you a war hero?" His reply was, "No, the heroes are the guys who didn't come home." That was the last I ever heard of the medals from my father who quietly put them back on the back shelf under the stairs in his workshop where they remained until his death 9 years later.

In 1979, I was in college and living on my own. The phone in my apartment rang on Friday, December 28 about 5:30 pm. It was my mom. She told me, "Get over here, something bad has happened to your father; I think he's had a heart attack." I remember the front door of our house being open. The front door was never open, that was a bad omen. There was an ambulance in the driveway and as I parked my car, I had a really bad feeling. I got to the top of the stairs in the house where I grew up and I saw my dad on the floor with two paramedics working furiously to revive him. Standing above him was Dr. Andy Gage, neighbor, family friend, and a pioneer in cardiac surgery. He looked me in the eye and slowly shook his head from side to side. His instinctive head nod told me, "Your father is dead."

My brother Phil, who is a military history buff, had requested my dad's service records from the Department of Defense. When they arrived we found out that my dad won a number of medals. Of greatest interest was the Distinguished Flying Cross, first awarded to Charles Lindbergh for heroism in flight. My dad was a war hero but never talked about his exploits. For him it was a private issue that he never brought up. I believe that his memories of the war were very painful and that he struggled with the fact that his crew may have inadvertently killed innocent women and children on their bombing runs. That thought secretly tortured him his entire life and silence was his retreat from that pain. He had talked briefly about using a hand ax to cut a 500 pound bomb loose from some cabling system but treated the incident as if he had changed spark plugs in the family car.

In 1991, our son Alex was born. He never met my dad, his grandfather, and I always felt bad about that fact. I knew both of my own grandfathers personally, and the legacy that they left to me. Alex knew nothing of his paternal grandfather other than what I had told him as he grew up. That wasn't enough for me.

Like all kids, I had always been drawn to motorcycles. My best childhood friend across the street had one that I wasn't supposed to ride. But I did ride it from time to time and as long as my mom didn't know, I was safe and secretly hooked on motorcycles. Twenty years went by and one night, around the time my dad died in December, I had a dream about creating a motorcycle that would honor my dad and his flight crew. I became obsessed with the idea and the details over the next year. I would wake up at night and draw up the plan in my head for what would become "Dinah Might"—a Harley Fatboy motorcycle patterned after my dad's B-29 from WWII. It would include the nose art from his plane on the gas tank, the 35 bombs painted on his plane signifying the 35 combat missions, the logo of the 20th Army Air Force, a Distinguished Flying Cross on the front fender and a depiction of the "Falling Man" from Rodin's sculpture "The Gates of Hell." My dad had worked in Paris, France for 9 months when I was young and he used to tell me, "As close as you'll ever come to falling into hell is going into combat."

I needed to be certain that we had our facts about the plane and the history correct, so I went on a data search. I included my son Alex, who at that time was 9 years old. We went on a mutual search for data on my dad's plane on the Internet and after we gathered our data, we submitted it to the historian for the 9th bomb group for authenticity. We found out that my dad's plane was the first B-29 to land on Iwo Jima on March 4 in 1945, two weeks after the Marines stormed the island and long before it was safe to land. The photo of that landing had been on the front page of *The New*

York Times and gave me the tail numbers for use on the bike.

We found out that my dad knew the crew members from the *Enola Gay*, the B-29 that dropped the first atomic bomb on Hiroshima that ended the war in the Pacific, and that my dad's plane was the next plane to take off right after the *Enola Gay* took off on its historic mission. My dad's plane was headed home while the *Enola Gay* was headed into the history books. I met with a crew member from my dad's plane in San Diego at the reunion of the 313th bomb group. I heard first-hand stories about my dad's calm demeanor under extreme pressure, his endless good humor, his curious whistling when the crew faced extreme pressure or enemy fire and his quiet valor that distinguished him above and beyond the common service man. We discovered a group of military photos, from the island of Tinian where my dad was stationed, for sale on eBay. This group of photos had been in an attic somewhere for over 50 years, and after I bought them for $22, we were stunned to find a close up face photo of my dad in his fatigues. The photo hangs in my office, a reminder to me that random chance is a powerful force.

Through our research and investigation, we found out that the Distinguished Flying Cross is one of the most important medals awarded by the Army Air Force for individual heroism in combat. I was able to show my son and solidify in my own mind that heroes are not pampered sports figures who play or refuse to play their childish games depending on their whim despite being offered millions of dollars each year. They are not rock or movie stars and they are not famous. They are much more than that. They are the folks who live next door who quietly respond to a call to duty in circumstances above and beyond most human comprehension. They went on to distinguish themselves in the face of brutal and terrifying circumstances. When they were done, there were no reporters, no huge contracts, no cameras, and no glory. They had done a horrible job extraordinarily well in the midst of great danger with no expectations beyond coming home alive. Could there be a greater or more sublime expectation than that?

Although my father died in 1979, he taught both the grandson he never met and his own sons the true meaning of heroism. Real heroism is quiet, gracious, subtle, and inexorably cemented to great honor, humility, and incredible inner strength. It is commonly a tale never told and details are found by luck and fortune frequently only after death, if ever at all. What greater legacy could a man leave to his sons and family than a private and personal view of valiant heroism?

Contributing Authors

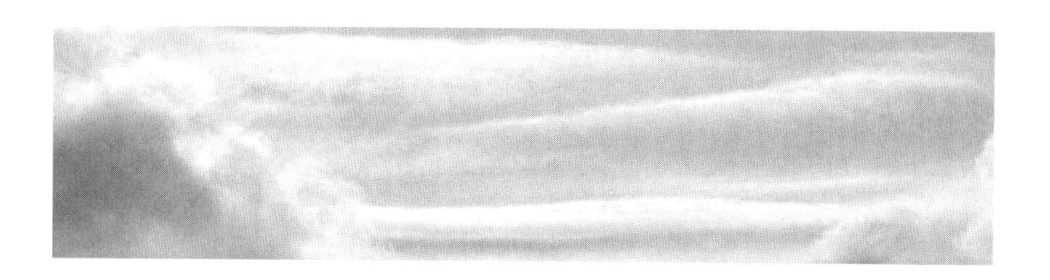

Linda Allen writes nonfiction and has been published in several magazines. She is the author of *Decking the Halls: The Folklore and Traditions of Christmas Plants.*

T. Jackson Anderson has won awards for his columns and been nominated for an Edgar award. He splits time between Monterey and Texas.

Patricia Asaad is a freelance newspaper and magazine writer living in Arlington, Texas. She writes everything from humor columns to touching essays about her family.

Julie Atkin, an actor and producer of film and theater, lives in Los Angeles. She founded Jewels Filmworks with her husband, Andrew Atkin.

Tom Basinski is a regional sales director for Biogen idec who resides in Getzville, New York. His written work has appeared in national publications and he credits his father and family for his success and zeal.

Renie Burghardt is a freelance writer who was born in Hungary. She has been published in many anthologies, including *Chicken Soup*, *Chocolate for Women*, *Guideposts*, *Cup of Comfort*, and many others.

Sal Amico M. Buttaci, an English teacher in New Jersey, has been writing and seeing his work in print since 1957. He owes it all to his parents.

Susan DeWolfe writes from Pearland, Texas (not quite in the Gulf of Mexico). Now retired, she writes essays and stories, and is working on three novels.

Gail Clanton Diggs, daughter of Gloria W. and the late George A. Clanton, is an executive marketing director in the Washington, D.C. area.

Thomas Edward has authored Technical Air Quality papers and other short stories, and won the American Express Gift Cheques' 4th Annual Humor Contest. His first book, *Stern's Reminder* is about the New Carissa incident.

Margaret A. Elliot, of Eliot, Maine, also writes fiction and poetry. She recently completed a book on Eliot for Arcadia Publishing's *Images of America* series.

Kristy Gillinder is a freelance writer who lives in Hilton Head Island, South Carolina. She enjoys sharing her love and her life with others through her writing.

Barbara Greenstreet, a writer and parenting consultant, has written articles for many publications. She writes and publishes the parenting newsletter, *Words of Wisdom*.

Mary Lou Healy is an author-essayist-poet, whose voice often reflects her New England country roots. Her most recent work is a novel of romantic suspense, *The Gingerbread Man*.

Gail Kavanagh lives in Queensland, Australia. Her writing has been published in *Scaifikuest, Arabella, Monthly Short Stories*, and *Women's Independent Press*, as well as the anthologies *Haunted Encounters*, *Changing Course* and *Simple Pleasures of the Kitchen*.

Eileen Key has published stories in *God Allows U Turns* and other publications. She writes book reviews and works as a proofreader for WestBow and Integrity Publishers.

Candy Killion, from South Florida, has also appeared in the *Chicken Soup, Rocking Chair Reader,* and *God Allows U-Turns* series.

Angie Klink, of Lafayette, Indiana, writes humorous and nostalgic essays about her two boys. Her children's book, *Purdue Pete Finds His Hammer*, will be published in 2005.

Leanne Krause is a graphic designer in Talent, Oregon. She's received a *Writer's Digest* Short Story Award and is currently working on her first novel.

Michele Lacina has been published in *The Philadelphia Inquirer, Country Woman* magazine, and *The Girls' Book of Success*. She is now pursuing her dream of publishing a novel.

Peter A. Land, MS, CSP, CMC, CPCM, is one of three people in the world to hold his earned professional credentials in speaking and consulting.

Dara Lehner resides in Ohio with Joe, her husband of twenty-three years, and their children and granddaughter. She writes children's mysteries, science, and inspirational books. Dara is also a photographer and speaker.

Kristine K. Lowder is an award-winning author residing in the Pacific Northwest. A graduate of Biola University, she is working on her next book.

Sharon McGonigal writes and teaches in Stony Plain, Alberta, Canada. Her stories have appeared in newspapers and as part of a historical anthology, and she's currently writing a non-fiction book for young adults set for publication in fall of 2006.

Mike Marinaro lives in Wendell, North Carolina. His writing has been published in Angels on Earth magazine and he is currently working on a book.

Dan Markham is a freelance writer from Indiana and the father of three children: Ian, Kiera, and Cormac.

Patricia Miller is a freelance writer living in Williamston, Michigan. She writes for regional publications, often about her family, the Great Lakes, and travel destinations.

Vanessa Lynn Moore, Clinical Psychologist, avid writer, and lover of all things literary, resides in her hometown of Washington, D.C.

Linda J. Parker is currently working on her third non-fiction book, *The Obvious Expert's Guide to Internet Marketing*. She and her family reside in Florida.

Tom Pawlak, resides in Chicago and is a professor of organizational design at Dominican University's Graduate School of Business. Tom frequently speaks on leadership effectiveness and its impact on business performance.

Nancy Robinson is a Connecticut-based writer, published internationally. An avid martial artist and former corporate professional, she writes about contemporary issues of the day.

Anne Roth travels across the country to teach creative writing workshops. She writes educational articles, children's books, and songs that enhance the creativity flowing within. She resides in Atlantic Beach, North Carolina and Franklinville, New Jersey.

Gregory J. Rummo is a syndicated columnist and author. His books are available from Amazon.com.

Annie Shapero currently resides in Rome, Italy, where she collaborates with WHERE Rome magazine, and continues her research for freelance travel articles.

Peri Shawn, known as the Executive Performance Coach, specializes in coaching and training sales executives. She is the author of the *Ultimate Sales Coaching with Integrity System.*

Jean Stewart writes history, travel, parenting, and family articles from her home in Mission Viejo, California. She is at work on two non-fiction books, one with her writers group.

Deborah Straw is a writer in Burlington, Vermont. Her books, *Natural Wonders of the Florida Keys* and *Why is Cancer Killing Our Pets?*, concern nature and animals.

Sharon Tabor Warren lives and writes in the shadows of the Virginia Blue Ridge. She's published articles, essays, creative nonfiction, and fiction; several of the latter have won awards. She credits her father with instilling in her the love of telling a story.

B.J. Taylor shares her home with three cats, one dog, and a wonderful husband. She is working on a book titled, *Find Your Dog a Job!* B.J. has had numerous stories published in magazines, newspapers and anthologies.

David Thatcher lives in Mississippi and works as an engineer. His son, Collin, is blessed by the lessons of the grandfather he never met.

Colleen Tillger is an aspiring writer living in the Philadelphia, Pennsylvania area. She writes personal and humorous essays, short stories, and is currently completing her first novel. Her father always encouraged her to pursue her dream of becoming a writer.

Shelagh Wulff-Wisdom lives in Douglas, Wyoming with her husband and horses. Her experiences as a rancher, horse trainer, and rodeo competitor provide the inspiration for her writing.

*About the OFWAIHF Founder and Creator of the **Who Art In Heaven**™ Series*

Gerry Murak, MS, MBA, is a Turnaround Performance Consultant, Executive Coach, founder of Murak and Associates, LLC, and has served as adjunct business faculty for the University of Buffalo, Cornell University School of Industrial and Labor Relations, and Daemen College. Gerry is also certified as a Professional in Human Resources Management. Currently he is a member of the Dean's Advisory Council for the University at Buffalo, School of Management.

Gerry is a member of the National Speakers Association and has given presentations in over thirty states, two Canadian provinces, and China where he has been nicknamed the "Enterprise Doctor." He is a past president of the Board of Directors for Upstate New York Turnaround Management Association, has published numerous business improvement articles, and is the recipient of several awards for leadership.

Gerry and his wife Barbara have been married for thirty-five years and live in Getzville, New York. They have two children and two grandsons who will come to know their late Great Grandfather through this book and the Our Fathers Who Art In Heaven Foundation (OFWAIHF) project, which Gerry founded in 2004.

www.OFWAIHF.org

who art in heaven™

SUBMIT YOUR STORIES

With the success of *Our Fathers Who Art In Heaven*, we are looking for other stories to complete new books in the series.

Did somebody you love teach you an important lesson about leadership or life that you still use today? What advice did your loved one give you that you still treasure?

Submit your stories today for the *Who Art In Heaven™* series. Send your favorite stories about your:

- Fathers Volume II
- Mothers
- Grandmothers
- Grandfathers
- Daughters
- Sons
- Children
- Spouses
- Godfathers
- Godmothers
- Sisters
- Brothers
- Aunts
- Uncles
- Relatives
- Parents
- In-Laws
- Friends
- Employees
- Co-workers
- Teachers
- Students
- Classmates
- Alumni
- Clergy
- Military
- Leaders
- Managers
- Coaches
- Neighbors

Submit stories to:
WAIH Publishing
PO Box 132
Getzville, NY 14068

Or E-mail your submissions to:
submissions@WAIHpublishing.com

For further information:
www.WAIHpublishing.com

WAIH Publishing
1-866-639-2443
info@WAIHpublishing.com

Our Fathers Who Art In Heaven
BOOK ORDERING INFORMATION

Online orders: http://www.murak.blogs.com/ourfatherswhoartinheaven

Telephone orders: 1-866-639-2443

Fax orders: 1-716-631-0257

Mail orders: WAIH Publishing, P.O. Box 132, Getzville, NY 14068

Our Fathers Who Art in Heaven **for $17.95 per copy (U.S. Funds)**

No. of books ______ Total purchase price ($17.95 per book): ________

Shipping and handling for the first book: $4.95

$2 (shipping and handling) for each additional copy: ________

Add sales tax for N.Y.S. orders: ________

Total enclosed: ________

Please Print Order Information

Name: ____________________

Address: ____________________

City: __________ State: __________ Zip: __________

Country: __________ Phone: __________

E-mail: ____________________

☐ Check/Money Order (make checks payable to: WAIH Publishing)

☐ VISA ☐ Master Card

Credit Card No.: __________ Exp. Date: __________

Cardholder Signature: ____________________

☐ I would like my book autographed.

☐ This book is a gift for: ____________________

Thank You!